FACES AT THE
BOTTOM OF THE WELL

FACES AT THE BOTTOM OF THE WELL

The Permanence of Racism

DERRICK BELL

BASIC BOOKS
New York

Basic Books
Hachette Book Group
1290 Avenue of the Americas, New York, NY 10104
www.basicbooks.com

Printed in the United States of America

First Edition: October 1992

Published by Basic Books, an imprint of Perseus Books, LLC, a subsidiary of Hachette Book Group, Inc. The Basic Books name and logo is a trademark of the Hachette Book Group.

The publisher is not responsible for websites (or their content) that are not owned by the publisher.

PRINT BOOK INTERIOR DESIGN BY JEFF WILLIAMS

Library of Congress Cataloging-in-Publication Data

Names: Bell, Derrick, 1930-2011.
Title: Faces at the bottom of the well : the permanence of racism / Derrick Bell.
Description: New York : Basic Books, 2018. | "First Edition: October 1992." | "With a new foreword by Michelle Alexander." | Includes bibliographical references and index.
Identifiers: LCCN 2018016457 (print) | LCCN 2018017053 (ebook) | ISBN 9781541645547 (ebook) | ISBN 9781541645530 (pbk.)
Subjects: LCSH: Racism--United States. | United States—Race relations. | African Americans--Civil rights.
Classification: LCC E185.615 (ebook) | LCC E185.615 .B395 2018 (print) | DDC 305.800973—dc23
LC record available at https://lccn.loc.gov/2018016457

ISBNs: 978-1-5416-4553-0 (paperback), 978-1-5416-4554-7 (ebook)

LSC-C

Printing 5, 2021

Black people are the magical faces at the bottom of society's well. Even the poorest whites, those who must live their lives only a few levels above, gain their self-esteem by gazing down on us. Surely, they must know that their deliverance depends on letting down their ropes. Only by working together is escape possible. Over time, many reach out, but most simply watch, mesmerized into maintaining their unspoken commitment to keeping us where we are, at whatever cost to them or to us.

D. B.

CONTENTS

FOREWORD

by Michelle Alexander

FEW LEGAL SCHOLARS IN RECENT MEMORY HAVE HAD A greater impact on racial justice thought and advocacy in the United States than Derrick Bell. I struggle to think of even one. Certainly no legal scholar has had a greater impact on me.

As a law student, I read nearly every word Bell wrote; as a civil rights lawyer, I was haunted by his words and ultimately forced to admit the truth of them; as a law professor, I insisted that my students read the very articles and books authored by Bell that had once been assigned to me.

I still have on my shelf the classic textbook entitled *Race, Racism, and American Law,* which Bell authored in 1971. That text became something like a bible for me when I was a law student, and I've carried it into every new work space

I enter. Eventually I wrote a book, *The New Jim Crow*, which would not have been possible but for Bell's scholarship and the contributions he made to the field of critical race theory—a body of legal scholarship that revolutionized what was spoken, taught, and debated in classrooms nationwide. Bell, along with other brilliant and visionary scholars, exposed the many ways in which racism is deeply embedded in our nation's laws and institutions, including many that are intended to remedy past injustices. I hardly stand alone in being profoundly influenced by Bell's scholarship as well as his courageous commitment to telling the truth, as best he could, about the realities of race in America.

The deep irony is that today Bell's name is not often spoken in legal and policy debates. His work is rarely cited by judges or legislators, and civil rights lawyers almost never claim to agree with his most famous and controversial thesis—the one that lies at the core of the book that you now hold in your hands: *Racism is permanent in the United States of America, utterly indestructible.*

The silence is hardly surprising. Civil rights lawyers, like myself, tend to cling to a more optimistic view. We want to believe that the right resources, legal strategies, political rhetoric, organizing campaigns, or media messaging will eventually transform this country into a thriving multiracial, multiethnic, egalitarian democracy. Lawyers of all stripes tend to want to imagine that we can solve, through law reform or litigation, the most vexing social problems. On our good days, we admit that we can't solve these problems alone. We point to our heroes and ancestors who sacrificed so much—often their very lives—to end slavery, lynching, and Jim Crow segregation. Didn't they prove Bell wrong? Didn't they prove that racial justice can be won? We call out their names: Ella Baker, Ida B. Wells, Martin Luther King Jr., Rosa Parks, Thurgood Marshall, and on and on. Thanks to their courage, we say, look how far we've come! We remind people that a mixed-race man named Barack Obama became president of the United States just forty years after the old Jim Crow system was brought to its knees. Doesn't Obama himself, the mere fact of him, prove Bell wrong? Just look at Obama! Well, don't look at him now that he's been replaced by a narcissistic Nazi sympathizer. Look at him in 2008. After centuries of slavery, followed by a hundred years of white terrorism and legal discrimination, the unimaginable happened: a multiracial, multiethnic, multiclass movement swept a black man into the highest office in the land. A movement that said, Yes We Can. Yes, we can make America what it must become.

And yet.

Reading Bell's words today, twenty-five years after the book was published, I find it difficult to refute the nuanced argument he weaves so gracefully—and unapologetically—in these pages. I read his words, and chills sweep over me. Something lurks in these pages that is eerily prophetic, almost haunting, and yet at the same time oddly reassuring. The truth about race and justice in America is always more liberating than the alternative.

No doubt there will be those who read this book and find it depressing, disturbing, foolish, or misguided, just as some people did back when it was first released. Some will mock or dismiss the allegories and parables. I remember being confused when I first read Bell's short stories as a law student. I was stunned not only by the content but also by the simplicity of the parables. Why would a renowned constitutional law scholar choose to write bizarre fictional dialogues involving an imaginary alter ego? Why were the stories written in such a simple, straightforward fashion using language an eighth grader could understand? Weren't law professors supposed to write stuff that only other academics could comprehend?

I will confess that I didn't fully appreciate the genius and power of these stories until I began discussing and debating them with others inside and outside classrooms. For many of my law school classmates—especially those of us who were black and brown—the parables functioned like a key to a secret door that we did not know had been locked within us. Once the door was opened, we found ourselves sharing our own stories, personal experiences with race and racism, including generational pain and trauma—many of which we had not had the courage to reveal before. And many of us began asking questions out loud that had been buried deep within us, locked away out of necessity or convenience or habit.

Back then, in 1992, when this book was originally released, the mere act of telling stories that challenged the assumption of neutrality in the law or that questioned the utility of law, litigation, or policy reform was deemed a radical, subversive act in many law schools. I was a student at Stanford

Law School at that time, and I remember well the battles that raged among faculty members, as well as students, regarding whether and to what extent Bell's claims (and the entire field of critical race theory) ought to be taken seriously.

Here we are, twenty-five years later. Bell's commitment to storytelling is no longer controversial in the legal academy. Women, Latinx, and queer scholars have found their voice in legal scholarship in no small part because of the doors Derrick Bell threw wide open. Yet just as Bell predicted, whatever progress has been made has been matched by devastating—downright disastrous—setbacks. Yes, the old Jim Crow system of legal segregation was officially ended by a carefully crafted legal campaign combined with an extraordinary, multiracial grassroots movement. But it is also true that less than two decades later public schools resegregated, and a new system of racial and social control was born in the United States—a system of mass incarceration that swept millions of poor people and people of color behind bars, quintupling our prison population, and relegated them to a permanent second-class status, stripping them of the very civil and human rights supposedly won in the Civil Rights Movement, including the right to vote, the right to serve on juries, and the right to be free of legal discrimination in employment, housing, access to education, and basic public benefits. In the words of Bryan Stevenson: "Slavery didn't end in 1865. It evolved."

A similar story can be told with respect to the election of Barack Obama to the presidency of the United States. Yes, it was a mind-blowing victory—a black man became president of the United States just forty years after "whites only" signs came down in public restrooms and black people were denied service at lunch counters throughout the South. And yet it is also true that people in the same states that proudly declared "segregation forever" in the 1950s came out in droves in 2016 to vote for Donald Trump by an overwhelming margin, throwing their support to a candidate who used precisely the same racially divisive political tactics that have successfully persuaded whites to choose their perceived racial interests over their economic interests since the days when this nation was founded. Over and over again, whites have shown a willingness to support the most brutal forms of racial oppression (or ignore them) while proudly calling themselves freedom-loving Christians. Our nation's perpetual civil war rages on.

Isn't it time we ask ourselves: What if Bell was right? What if justice for the dark faces at "the bottom of the well" can't actually be won in the United States? What if all "progress" toward racial justice is illusory, temporary, and inevitably unstable? What if white supremacy will always rebound, finding new ways to reconstitute itself?

What if racism is permanent? What if?

There was a time in my life when I resisted those questions, sometimes laughing them off. It wasn't that I didn't take Derrick Bell, as a scholar, seriously. To the contrary, I was already in awe of his work before *Faces at the Bottom of the Well* burst onto the scene. Not only was his textbook a primary resource for me, but his seminal article, "Serving Two Masters: Integration Ideals and Client Interests in

School Desegregation Litigation," had profoundly altered my understanding of what kind of civil rights lawyer I wanted to become. Bell argued convincingly in that piece that civil rights lawyers at the NAACP Legal Defense Fund—where he himself had worked—effectively sold out their clients in school desegregation cases by pursuing racial integration instead of quality of education, overriding the preferences of their clients because of the lawyers' ideological commitment to integration and pressure from wealthy donors and foundations. That article left me determined to become a different kind of civil rights lawyer. I would not betray the communities that I claimed to represent, and I would not allow funders and financial concerns to influence my law practice. Only later would I come to realize how much easier that is said than done.

Even if we set aside his scholarship, Derrick Bell was a legendary figure in the legal academy when *Faces at the Bottom of the Well* was released. He was the first African American tenured by Harvard Law School—a striking accomplishment in itself—but, more importantly, he was the first to quit a law faculty in protest of discriminatory hiring practices. In 1990, Bell shocked his colleagues by launching a protest that included a hunger strike and sit-ins, followed by an announcement that he was taking an unpaid leave of absence from the faculty, vowing not to return until the law school hired, for the first time, a black woman to join its tenured faculty. His decision to walk away from Harvard Law School in protest made the national news, sparking controversy on campuses from coast to coast and helping to bolster organizing efforts aimed at diversifying law school faculties—efforts I was participating in as a student at Stanford. A young Barack Obama, while a law student at Harvard, compared Bell to Rosa Parks.

This is a long way of saying that my laughter was not a sign that I didn't care what Bell had to say. To the contrary, it was a coping mechanism, a way of avoiding the implications of his thesis. I couldn't help but wonder: If racism is permanent, then what is the point of the struggle? His suggestion that meaning and purpose could be derived from the mere act of resistance rang hollow for me. I wanted to make a difference, bring us closer to Martin Luther King Jr.'s dream, and yet Bell seemed to say that King's dream was nothing more than a fantasy.

Faces at the Bottom of the Well challenged nearly every assumption I had, as an aspiring civil rights lawyer, about what I could reasonably expect to accomplish if I continued down my chosen path. Any temptation I might have felt to dismiss Bell as an untrustworthy messenger—as someone whose motivations were suspect or who lacked relevant life experience—was undermined by the fact that he, like me, went to law school imagining that he could help "win" justice for black Americans through legal battles and carefully crafted organizing and political strategies. Bell had dedicated many years of his life to precisely the type of civil rights litigation and advocacy that I hoped to do in the world—litigation challenging race discrimination in schooling, housing, voting, and much more. He had worked alongside many of my heroes, like Thurgood Marshall, and he had been in the trenches before he entered the ivory tower, representing civil rights activists who were on the front lines of the black freedom struggle. Now here he was, writing stories suggesting that nothing that any of us might do inside or outside courtrooms would ever change, in the long run, the political calculus for white Americans. Black interests, he said, will always be sacrificed for white gain.

That point was made most dramatically in "The Space Traders," the parable that would eventually become one of Bell's most widely discussed and debated pieces of writing. In the story, aliens from another planet visit Earth and offer the United States enough gold to eliminate the national debt, a magic chemical that would eliminate all pollution, and an unlimited source of safe energy. In exchange, the aliens wanted only one thing in return: America's entire black population, which would be taken to outer space. After some hand-wringing, the white population accepts the offer by a huge margin. And off we go.

I do not recall discussing this story with any black person—not one—who doubted that things would go down precisely that way in real life. None of us questioned the outcome. What we argued about was whether there was any hope that white people could be persuaded, one day, to make a different choice.

Throughout all of the parables in this book, Bell advanced his "interest convergence theory," the idea that whites have never (and would never) support efforts to improve the position of black Americans unless it was in their interest to do so. Bell seemed to suggest that the best we could do, as racial justice advocates, is seek to mitigate the harms of white supremacy and take full advantage of the moments in which whites could see that their interests were aligned with our own, recognizing that these moments would rarely last for long. We should be prepared not only for the likely backlash against any signs of black progress but also for the likelihood that any remedies for injustice would operate to perpetuate the racial hierarchy in the long run. Racism in this country is permanent, he insisted, no matter what we say or do.

To say this argument was difficult for many of us to swallow is an understatement. I graduated from law school grateful for what Bell had taught me but determined to prove him wrong.

Reading this book again, after so much has changed and so much has remained the same in this country, I no longer fear the possibility that Bell may well be right. I now understand that accepting the permanence of racism in this country does not mean accepting racism. It does not mean being a passive spectator as politicians engage in racial scapegoating. It does not mean doing nothing as our nation builds a border wall locking some colored people out, while building prison walls that lock millions of others in. Accepting the permanence of racism does not mean ignoring global capitalism and the many ways in which it treats millions of people and the planet itself as expendable, utterly disposable. Accepting the permanence of racism does not mean denying or avoiding sexism and patriarchy.

Facing the inconvenient truth that America may suffer from an incurable, potentially fatal disease helps to clarify what we're up against. It offers the opportunity to clarify our goals. Is our ultimate goal to save this nation from its original sins? Are we trying to "fix" the United States of America? If so, Bell rightly argues that we may find ourselves playing a game we can never win. But if we broaden our view and sharpen our focus, we just might see that our liberation struggles aren't limited to our national borders and that our movements, if we take them seriously enough, can help to rebirth this nation and reimagine our world. A new country might be born, one with new heroes, new founding mothers and fathers. I don't expect to live long enough to see that day, and I won't pretend to be certain that it will come. What I do know is that none of us can say for sure what will happen when the seeds planted by today's truth tellers and advocates begin to sprout and bloom. Perhaps our movements—the rebellious spirit that gives life to them—will outlive this country and help to make another world possible.

Whether you believe our nation can be saved or redeemed, I urge you to read (or reread) this book and discuss it with others. Ask yourself whether there may be truths lurking here that we have yet to face. Ask yourself if you're willing to commit yourself to the struggle for racial justice even if the battle can't ever be won. After years of ambivalence on that final point, my answer now is yes. Forever yes.

PREFACE

AT THE OUTSET, LET ME ASSURE HER MANY FRIENDS THAT the lawyer-prophet Geneva Crenshaw, the fictional heroine of *And We Are Not Saved: The Elusive Quest for Racial Justice,* has returned. In that earlier book, through a series of allegorical stories, she and I discussed the workings—and the failures—of civil rights laws and policies. Here, I again enlist the use of literary models as a more helpful vehicle than legal precedent in a continuing quest for new directions in our struggle for racial justice, a struggle we must continue even if—as I contend here—racism is an integral, permanent, and indestructible component of this society.

The challenge throughout has been to tell what I view as the truth about racism without causing disabling despair. For some of us who bear the burdens of racial subordination, any truth—no matter how dire—is uplifting. For others, it may be reassuring to remember Paulo Freire's words: "Freedom is acquired by conquest, not by gift. It must be pursued constantly and responsibly. Freedom is not an ideal located outside of . . . [the individual]; nor is it an idea which becomes myth. It is rather the indispensable condition for the quest for human completion."[1]

Albert Camus, too, saw the need for struggle even in the face of certain defeat: "Man is mortal. That may be; but let us die resisting; and if our lot is complete annihilation, let us not behave in such a way that it seems justice!"[2] In a similar vein, Franz Fanon conceded that "I as a man of color do not have the right to hope that in the white man there will be a crystallization of guilt toward the past of my race. . . . My life [as a Negro] is caught in the lasso of existence. . . . I find myself suddenly in the world and I recognize that I have one right alone: that of demanding human behavior from the other. One duty alone: that of not renouncing my freedom through my choices."[3]

Fanon argued two seemingly irreconcilable points, and insisted on both. On the one hand, he believed racist structures to be permanently embedded in the psychology, economy, society, and culture of the modern world—so much so that he expressed the belief "that a true culture cannot come to life under present conditions."[4] But, on the other hand, he urged people of color to resist psychologically the inheritance they had come into. He insisted, despite pages of evidence suggesting the inviolability of the racial order, that "I should constantly *remind myself* that the real *leap* consists in introducing invention into existence. For the world through which I travel, I am endlessly creating myself."[5]

Fanon's book was enormously pessimistic in a *victory* sense. He did not believe that modern structures, deeply poisoned with racism, could be overthrown. And yet he urged resistance. He wrote a book—perhaps to remind himself that material or cultural fate is only part of the story.

While Martin Luther King spoke much about racial justice in integrationist terms, in an essay, *A Testament of Hope*, published after his death, he wrote of his setbacks, the time he spent in jails, his frustrations and sorrows, and the dangerous character of his adversaries. He said those adversaries expected him to harden into a grim and desperate man. But: "They fail, however, to perceive the sense of affirmation generated by the challenge of embracing struggle and surmounting obstacles."[6] So, while Dr. King led a struggle toward a goal—racial equality—that seemed possible, if not quite feasible, in the 1960s, there was a deeper message of commitment to courageous struggle whatever the circumstances or the odds. A part of that struggle was the need to speak the truth as he viewed it even when that truth alienated rather than unified, upset minds rather than calmed hearts, and subjected the speaker to general censure rather than acclaim.

Statements of faith by men who had thought deeply about the problems of human life, whether white or black, encouraged me in writing this book. And I was moved and motivated by the courageous example of the many black people with whom I worked in the South during my years as a civil rights lawyer. Judge Robert L. Carter, one of the leading attorneys in the NAACP's school desegregation litigation, has spoken of this courage when, back in the early 1950s, whites exerted economic pressures to curb the new militancy among blacks who were joining lawsuits challenging segregation. In that climate, Carter and the other lawyers urged parents to consider carefully the risks before making a final commitment to join in the litigation. "That so few stepped back still astounds me," says Carter.[7]

Carter's observation takes me back to the summer of 1964. It was a quiet, heat-hushed evening in Harmony, a small black community near the Mississippi Delta. Some Harmony residents, in the face of increasing white hostility, were organizing to ensure implementation of a court order mandating desegregation of their schools the next September. Walking with her up a dusty, unpaved road toward her modest home, I asked one of the organizers, Mrs. Biona MacDonald, where she and the other black families found the courage to continue working for civil rights in the face of intimidation that included blacks losing their jobs, the local banks trying to foreclose on the mortgages of those active in the civil rights movement, and shots fired through their windows late at night.

Mrs. MacDonald looked at me and said slowly, seriously, "I can't speak for everyone, but as for me, I am an old woman. I lives to harass white folks."

Since then, I have thought a lot about Mrs. MacDonald and those other courageous black folk in Leake County, Mississippi, particularly Dovie and Winson Hudson. Remembering again that long-ago conversation, I realized that Mrs. MacDonald didn't say she risked everything because she hoped or expected to win out over the whites who, as she well knew, held all the economic and political power, and the guns as well. Rather, she recognized that—powerless as she was—she had and intended to use courage and determination as a weapon to, in her words, "harass white folks."

As I do throughout this book, Mrs. MacDonald assumed that I knew that not all whites are racist, but that the oppression she was committed to resist was racial and emanated from whites. She did not even hint that her harassment would topple those whites' well-entrenched power. Rather, her goal was defiance, and its harassing effect was likely more potent precisely because she did what she did without expecting to topple her oppressors. Mrs. MacDonald avoided discouragement and defeat because at the point that she determined to resist her oppression, she was triumphant. Her answer to my question reflected the value of that triumph, explained the source of courage that fueled her dangerous challenge to the white power structure of that rural Mississippi county. Nothing the all-powerful whites could do to her would diminish her triumph.

———

THIS BOOK'S UNORTHODOX form is a testament to the support and the persistence of Martin Kessler, president and editorial director of Basic Books. For her assistance as well as valuable ideas and editing help, I owe a real debt to my former student Erin Edmonds, J.D., Harvard '91, a demon writer in her own right. The interweaving of fact and fiction requires writing skill and experience possessed by few law teachers, including this author. To fill the gap between idea and execution, I relied on Basic Books's development editor Phoebe Hoss, who here, as she did in *And We Are Not Saved,* labored far beyond the awesome obligations of her unsung profession to give these chapters intelligible form and logical structure.

Lynn Walker, the director of the Ford Foundation's Human Rights and Social Justice Programs, provided a grant that helped with research assistance. I also received a grant from the Harvard Law School's summer research program. Earlier versions of some of these stories were written for and discussed with my Civil Rights at the Crossroads Seminars at the Harvard Law School in 1989 and 1990. My thanks to the many persons who read all or portions of this manuscript. They include: Anita Allen, Karen Beckwith, Carter Bell, Arlene Brock, Janet Dewart, Dagmar Miller, Cindy Monaco, Linda Singer, Krenie Stowe, Sung-Hee Suh, and Ayelet Waldman. John Hayakawa Torok helped with research, and Dan Gunnells, Michelle Degree, and Cheryl Jackson performed various secretarial functions.

Several of the stories were written to facilitate classroom discussion. Some were then published elsewhere, usually in substantially different versions, and I gratefully acknowledge permission to reprint them: Chapter 1, "Racial Symbols: A Limited Legacy" in "A Holiday for Dr. King: The Significance of Symbols in the Black Freedom Struggle," *University of California at Davis Law Review* 17 (1983): 433; chapter 3, "The Racial Preference Licensing Act," in "Foreword: The Final Civil Rights Act," *California Law Review* 79 (1991):

597; chapter 4, "The Last Black Hero," in "The Last Black Hero," *Harvard Blackletter Law Journal* 8 (1991): 51; chapter 5, "Divining a Racial Realism Theory," in "Xerces and the Affirmative Action Mystique (A Tribute to Professor Arthur S. Miller)," 57 *George Washington Law Review* 1595 (1989): 701; chapter 6, "The Rules of Racial Standing," in "The Law of Racial Standing," *Yale Journal of Law and Liberation* 2 (1991): 117; chapter 9, "The Space Traders," in "A Forum on Derrick Bell's Civil Rights Chronicles," 1989 Sanford E. Sarasohn Memorial Lecture, *St. Louis University Law Journal* 34 (1990): 393; and in "Racism: A Prophecy for the Year 2000," *Rutgers Law Review* 42 (1989): 1.

Divining Our Racial Themes

In these bloody days and frightful nights when an
urban warrior can find no face more despicable
than his own, no ammunition more deadly than
self-hate and no target more deserving of his true
aim than his brother, we must wonder how we
came so late and lonely to this place.

—Maya Angelou

WHEN I WAS GROWING UP IN THE YEARS BEFORE THE
Second World War, our slave heritage was more a
symbol of shame than a source of pride. It burdened black
people with an indelible mark of difference as we struggled
to be like whites. In those far-off days, survival and progress seemed to require moving beyond, even rejecting slavery. Childhood friends in a West Indian family who lived
a few doors away often boasted—erroneously as I later
learned—that their people had never been slaves. My own

more accurate—but hardly more praiseworthy—response was that my forebears included many free Negroes, some of whom had Choctaw and Blackfoot Indian blood.

In those days, self-delusion was both easy and comforting. Slavery was barely mentioned in the schools and seldom discussed by the descendants of its survivors, particularly those who had somehow moved themselves to the North. Emigration, whether from the Caribbean islands or from the Deep South states, provided a geographical distance that encouraged and enhanced individual denial of our collective, slave past. We sang spirituals but detached the songs from their slave origins. As I look back, I see this reaction as no less sad, for being very understandable. We were a subordinate and mostly shunned portion of a society that managed to lay the onus of slavery neatly on those who were slaves while simultaneously exonerating those who were slaveholders. All things considered, it seemed a history best left alone.

Then, after the Second World War and particularly in the 1960s, slavery became—for a few academics and some militant Negroes—a subject of fascination and a sure means of evoking racial rage as a prelude to righteously repeated demands for "Freedom Now!" In response to a resurrection of interest in our past, new books on slavery were written, long out-of-print volumes republished. The new awareness reached its highest point in 1977 with the television version of Alex Haley's biographical novel, *Roots*.[1] The highly successful miniseries informed millions of Americans—black as well as white—that slavery in fact existed and that it was awful. Not, of course, as awful as it would have been save for the good white folks the television writers had created to ease the slaves' anguish, and the evil ones on whose shoulders they placed all the guilt. Through the magic of literary license, white viewers could feel revulsion for slavery without necessarily recognizing American slavery as a burden on the nation's history, certainly not a burden requiring reparations in the present.

Even so, under pressure of civil rights protests, many white Americans were ready to accede to if not applaud Supreme Court rulings that the Constitution should no longer recognize and validate laws that kept in place the odious badges of slavery.

As a result, two centuries after the Constitution's adoption, we did live in a far more enlightened world. Slavery was no more. Judicial precedent and a plethora of civil rights statutes formally prohibited racial discrimination. Compliance was far from perfect, but the slavery provisions in the Constitution* did seem lamentable artifacts of a less enlightened era.

But the fact of slavery refuses to fade, along with the deeply embedded personal attitudes and public policy assumptions that supported it for so long. Indeed, the racism that made slavery feasible is far from dead in the last decade of twentieth-century America; and the civil rights gains, so hard won, are being steadily eroded. Despite undeniable progress for many, no African Americans are insulated from incidents of racial discrimination. Our careers, even our

---

* According to William Wiecek, ten provisions in the Constitution directly or indirectly provided for slavery and protected slave owners.[2]

lives, are threatened because of our color. Even the most successful of us are haunted by the plight of our less fortunate brethren who struggle for existence in what some social scientists call the "underclass." Burdened with life-long poverty and soul-devastating despair, they live beyond the pale of the American Dream. What we designate as "racial progress" is not a solution to that problem. It is a regeneration of the problem in a particularly perverse form.

According to data compiled in 1990 for basic measures of poverty, unemployment, and income, the slow advances African Americans made during the 1960s and 1970s have definitely been reversed. The unemployment rate for blacks is 2.5 times the rate for whites. Black per-capita income is not even two thirds of the income for whites; and blacks, most of whom own little wealth or business property, are three times more likely to have income below the poverty level than whites.[3] If trends of the last two decades are allowed to continue, readers can safely—and sadly—assume that the current figures are worse than those cited here.*

Statistics cannot, however, begin to express the havoc caused by joblessness and poverty: broken homes, anarchy in communities, futility in the public schools. All are the

---

* Not all the data are bleak. While the median family income for black families declined in the 1970s and 1980s, the proportion of African-American families with incomes of $35,000 to $50,000 increased from 23.3 to 27.5 percent. The proportion with incomes above $50,000 increased by 38 percent, from 10.0 to 13.8 percent. The overall median income for blacks declined though: while the top quarter made progress, the bottom half was sliding backward, and the proportion of blacks receiving very low income (less than $5,000) actually increased.[4]

bitter harvest of race-determined unemployment in a society where work provides sustenance, status, and the all-important sense of self-worth. What we now call the "inner city" is, in fact, the American equivalent of the South African homelands. Poverty is less the source than the status of men and women who, despised because of their race, seek refuge in self-rejection. Drug-related crime, teenaged parenthood, and disrupted and disrupting family life all are manifestations of a despair that feeds on self. That despair is bred anew each day by the images on ever-playing television sets, images confirming that theirs is the disgraceful form of living, not the only way people live.

Few whites are able to identify with blacks as a group—the essential prerequisite for feeling empathy with, rather than aversion from, blacks' self-inflicted suffering, as expressed by the poet Maya Angelou in this Introduction's epigraph. Unable or unwilling to perceive that "there but for the grace of God, go I," few whites are ready to actively promote civil rights for blacks. Because of an irrational but easily roused fear that any social reform will unjustly benefit blacks, whites fail to support the programs this country desperately needs to address the ever-widening gap between the rich and the poor, both black and white.

Lulled by comforting racial stereotypes, fearful that blacks will unfairly get ahead of them, all too many whites respond to even the most dire reports of race-based disadvantage with either a sympathetic headshake or victim-blaming rationalizations. Both responses lead easily to the conclusion that contemporary complaints of racial discrimination are simply excuses put forward by people who are unable or unwilling to compete on an equal basis in a competitive society.

For white people who both deny racism and see a heavy dose of the Horatio Alger myth as the answer to blacks' problems, how sweet it must be when a black person stands in a public place and condemns as slothful and unambitious those blacks who are not making it. Whites eagerly embrace black conservatives' homilies to self-help, however grossly unrealistic such messages are in an economy where millions, white as well as black, are unemployed and, more important, in one where racial discrimination in the workplace is as vicious (if less obvious) than it was when employers posted signs "no negras need apply."

Whatever the relief from responsibility such thinking provides those who embrace it, more than a decade of civil rights setbacks in the White House, in the courts, and in the critical realm of media-nurtured public opinion has forced retrenchment in the tattered civil rights ranks. We must reassess our cause and our approach to it, but repetition of time-worn slogans simply will not do. As a popular colloquialism puts it, it is time to "get real" about race and the persistence of racism in America.

To make such an assessment—to plan for the future by reviewing the experiences of the past—we must ask whether the formidable hurdles we now face in the elusive quest for racial equality are simply a challenge to our commitment, whether they are the latest variation of the old hymn "One More River to Cross." Or, as we once again gear up to meet the challenges posed by these unexpected new setbacks, are we ignoring a current message with implications for the future which history has already taught us about the past?

Such assessment is hard to make. On the one hand, contemporary color barriers are certainly less visible as a result of our successful effort to strip the law's endorsement from the hated Jim Crow signs. Today one can travel for thousands of miles across this country and never see a public facility designated as "Colored" or "White." Indeed, the very absence of visible signs of discrimination creates an atmosphere of racial neutrality and encourages whites to believe that racism is a thing of the past. On the other hand, the general use of so-called neutral standards to continue exclusionary practices reduces the effectiveness of traditional civil rights laws, while rendering discriminatory actions more oppressive than ever. Racial bias in the *pre-Brown* era was stark, open, unalloyed with hypocrisy and blank-faced lies. We blacks, when rejected, knew who our enemies were. They were not us! Today, because bias is masked in unofficial practices and "neutral" standards, we must wrestle with the question whether race or some individual failing has cost us the job, denied us the promotion, or prompted our being rejected as tenants for an apartment. Either conclusion breeds frustration and alienation—and a rage we dare not show to others or admit to ourselves.

Modern discrimination is, moreover, not practiced indiscriminately. Whites, ready and willing to applaud, even idolize black athletes and entertainers, refuse to hire, or balk at working with, blacks. Whites who number individual blacks among their closest friends approve, or do not oppose, practices that bar selling or renting homes or apartments in their neighborhoods to blacks they don't know. Employers, not wanting "too many of them," are willing to hire one or two black people, but will reject those who apply later. Most hotels and restaurants who offer black patrons courteous— even deferential—treatment, uniformly reject black job applicants, except perhaps for the most menial jobs. When did you last see a black waiter in a really good restaurant?

Racial schizophrenia is not limited to hotels and restaurants. As a result, neither professional status nor relatively high income protects even accomplished blacks from capricious acts of discrimination that may reflect either individual "preference" or an institution's bias. The motivations for bias vary; the disadvantage to black victims is the same.

Careful examination reveals a pattern to these seemingly arbitrary racial actions. When whites perceive that it will be profitable or at least cost-free to serve, hire, admit, or otherwise deal with blacks on a nondiscriminatory basis, they do so. When they fear—accurately or not—that there may be a loss, inconvenience, or upset to themselves or other whites, discriminatory conduct usually follows. Selections and rejections reflect preference as much as prejudice. A preference for whites makes it harder to prove the discrimination outlawed by civil rights laws. This difficulty, when combined with lackluster enforcement, explains why discrimination in employment and in the housing market continues to prevail more than two decades after enactment of the Equal Employment Opportunity Act of 1965[5] and the Fair Housing Act of 1968.[6]

Racial policy is the culmination of thousands of these individual practices. Black people, then, are caught in a double bind. We are, as I have said, disadvantaged unless whites perceive that nondiscriminatory treatment for us will be a benefit for them. In addition, even when nonracist practices might bring a benefit, whites may rely on discrimination against blacks as a unifying factor and a safety valve for frustrations during economic hard times.

Almost always, the injustices that dramatically diminish the rights of blacks are linked to the serious economic disadvantage suffered by many whites who lack money and power. Whites, rather than acknowledge the similarity of their disadvantage, particularly when compared with that of better-off whites, are easily detoured into protecting their sense of entitlement vis-à-vis blacks for all things of value. Evidently, this racial preference expectation is hypnotic. It is this compulsive fascination that seems to prevent most whites from even seeing—much less resenting—the far more sizable gap between their status and those who occupy the lofty levels at the top of our society.

Race consciousness of this character, as Professor Kimberlè Crenshaw suggested in 1988 in a pathbreaking *Harvard Law Review* article, makes it difficult for whites "to imagine the world differently. It also creates the desire for identification with privileged elites. By focusing on a distinct, subordinate 'other,' whites include themselves in the dominant circle—an arena in which most hold no real power, but only their privileged racial identity."[7]

The critically important stabilizing role that blacks play in this society constitutes a major barrier in the way of achieving racial equality. Throughout history, politicians have used blacks as scapegoats for failed economic or political policies. Before the Civil War, rich slave owners persuaded the white working class to stand with them against the danger of slave revolts—even though the existence of slavery condemned white workers to a life of economic privation.[8] After the Civil War, poor whites fought social reforms and settled for segregation rather than see formerly enslaved blacks get ahead.[9] Most labor unions preferred to allow plant owners to break strikes with black scab labor than allow blacks to join their ranks.[10] The "them against us" racial ploy—always a potent force in economic bad times—is working again: today whites, as disadvantaged by high-status entrance requirements as blacks, fight to end affirmative action policies that, by eliminating class-based entrance requirements and requiring widespread advertising of jobs, have likely helped far more whites than blacks. And in the 1990s, as through much of the 1980s, millions of Americans—white as well as black—face steadily worsening conditions: unemployment, inaccessible health care, inadequate housing, mediocre education, and pollution of the environment. The gap in national incomes is approaching a crisis as those in the top fifth now earn more than their counterparts in the bottom four fifths combined. The conservative guru Kevin Phillips used a different but no less disturbing comparison: the top two million income earners in this country earn more than the next one hundred million.[11]

Shocking. And yet conservative white politicians are able to gain and hold even the highest office despite their failure to address seriously any of these issues. They rely instead on the time-tested formula of getting needy whites to identify on the basis of their shared skin color, and suggest with little or no subtlety that white people must stand together against the Willie Hortons, or against racial quotas, or against affirmative action. The code words differ. The message is the same. Whites are rallied on the basis of racial pride and patriotism to accept their often lowly lot in life, and encouraged to vent their frustration by opposing any serious advancement by blacks. Crucial to this situation is the unstated understanding by the mass of whites that they will accept large disparities in economic opportunity in respect to other whites as long as they have a priority over blacks and other people of color for access to the few opportunities available.

This "racial bonding" by whites[12] means that black rights and interests are always vulnerable to diminishment if not to outright destruction. The willingness of whites over time to respond to this racial rallying cry explains—far more than does the failure of liberal democratic practices (regarding black rights) to coincide with liberal democratic theory—blacks' continuing subordinate status. This is, of course, contrary to the philosophy of Gunnar Myrdal's massive midcentury study *An American Dilemma*. Myrdal and two generations of civil rights advocates accepted the idea of racism as merely an odious holdover from slavery, "a terrible and inexplicable anomaly stuck in the middle of our liberal democratic ethos."[13] No one doubted that the standard American policy making was adequate to the task of abolishing racism. White America, it was assumed, *wanted* to abolish racism.*

Forty years later, in *The New American Dilemma*, Professor Jennifer Hochschild examined what she called Myrdal's "anomaly thesis," and concluded that it simply cannot explain the persistence of racial discrimination.[15] Rather, the continued viability of racism demonstrates "that racism is not simply an excrescence on a fundamentally healthy liberal democratic body, but is part of what shapes and energizes the body."[16] Under this view, "liberal democracy and racism in the United States are historically, even inherently, reinforcing; American society as we know it exists only because of its foundation in racially based slavery, and it thrives only because racial discrimination continues. The apparent anomaly is an actual symbiosis."[17]

The permanence of this "symbiosis" ensures that civil rights gains will be temporary and setbacks inevitable. Consider: In this last decade of the twentieth century, color determines the social and economic status of all African Americans, both those who have been highly successful and their poverty-bound brethren whose lives are grounded in misery and despair. We rise and fall less as a result of our

---

* According to Myrdal, the "Negro problem in America represents a moral lag in the development of the nation and a study of it must record nearly everything which is bad and wrong in America. . . . However, . . . not since Reconstruction has there been more reason to anticipate fundamental changes in American race relations, changes which will involve a development toward the American ideals."[14]

efforts than in response to the needs of a white society that condemns all blacks to quasi citizenship as surely as it segregated our parents and enslaved their forebears. The fact is that, despite what we designate as progress wrought through struggle over many generations, we remain what we were in the beginning: a dark and foreign presence, always the designated "other." Tolerated in good times, despised when things go wrong, as a people we are scapegoated and sacrificed as distraction or catalyst for compromise to facilitate resolution of political differences or relieve economic adversity.

We are now, as were our forebears when they were brought to the New World, objects of barter for those who, while profiting from our existence, deny our humanity. It is in the light of this fact that we must consider the haunting questions about slavery and exploitation contained in Professor Linda Myers's *Understanding an Afrocentric World View: Introduction to an Optimal Psychology*, questions that serve as their own answers.[18]

We simply cannot prepare realistically for our future without assessing honestly our past. It seems cold, accusatory, but we must try to fathom with her "the mentality of a people that could continue for over 300 years to kidnap an estimated 50 million youth and young adults from Africa, transport them across the Atlantic with about half dying unable to withstand the inhumanity of the passage, and enslave them as animals."[19]

As Professor Myers reminds us, blacks were not the only, and certainly not America's most, persecuted people. Appropriately, she asks about the mindset of European Americans to native Americans. After all, those in possession of the land were basically friendly to the newcomers. And yet the European Americans proceeded to annihilate almost the entire race, ultimately forcing the survivors onto reservations after stealing their land. Far from acknowledging and atoning for these atrocities, American history portrays whites as the heroes, the Indian victims as savage villains. "What," she wonders, "can be understood about the world view of a people who claim to be building a democracy with freedom and justice for all, and at the same time own slaves and deny others basic human rights?"[20]

Of course, Americans did not invent slavery. The practice has existed throughout recorded history, and Professor Orlando Patterson, a respected scholar, argues impressively that American slavery was no worse than that practiced in other parts of the world.* But it is not comparative slavery policies that concern me. Slavery is, as an example of what white America has done, a constant reminder of what white America might do.

We must see this country's history of slavery, not as an insuperable racial barrier to blacks, but as a legacy of enlightenment from our enslaved forebears reminding us that if they survived the ultimate form of racism, we and those whites who stand with us can at least view racial oppression

---

* He suggests: "The dishonor of slavery . . . came in the primal act of submission. It was the most immediate human expression of the inability to defend oneself or to secure one's livelihood. . . . The dishonor the slave was compelled to experience sprang instead from that raw, human sense of debasement inherent in having no being except as an expression of another's being."[21]

in its many contemporary forms without underestimating its critical importance and likely permanent status in this country.

To initiate the reconsideration, I want to set forth this proposition, which will be easier to reject than refute: *Black people will never gain full equality in this country. Even those herculean efforts we hail as successful will produce no more than temporary "peaks of progress," short-lived victories that slide into irrelevance as racial patterns adapt in ways that maintain white dominance. This is a hard-to-accept fact that all history verifies. We must acknowledge it, not as a sign of submission, but as an act of ultimate defiance.*

We identify with and hail as hero the man or woman willing to face even death without flinching.[22] Why? Because, while no one escapes death, those who conquer their dread of it are freed to live more fully. In similar fashion, African Americans must confront and conquer the otherwise deadening reality of our permanent subordinate status. Only in this way can we prevent ourselves from being dragged down by society's racial hostility. Beyond survival lies the potential to perceive more clearly both a reason and the means for further struggle.

In this book, Geneva Crenshaw, the civil rights lawyer–protagonist of my earlier *And We Are Not Saved: The Elusive Quest for Racial Justice,* returns in a series of stories that offer an allegorical perspective on old dreams, long-held fears, and current conditions. The provocative format of story, a product of experience and imagination, allows me to take a new look at what, for want of a better phrase,

I will call "racial themes." Easier to recognize than describe, they are essentials in the baggage of people subordinated by color in a land that boasts of individual freedom and equality. Some of these themes—reliance on law, involvement in protests, belief in freedom symbols—are familiar and generally known. Others—the yearning for a true homeland, the rejection of racial testimony, the temptation to violent retaliation—are real but seldom revealed. Revelation does not much alter the mystique of interracial romance or lessen its feared consequences. Nor does the search ever end for a full understanding of why blacks are and remain this country's designated scapegoats.

Everpresent, always lurking in the shadow of current events, is the real possibility that an unexpected coincidence of events at some point in the future—like those that occurred in the past—will persuade whites to reach a consensus that a major benefit to the nation justifies an ultimate sacrifice of black rights—or lives. Chapter 9 portrays one such fictional coincidence in "The Space Traders." By concluding the book on this dire note, I hope to emphasize the necessity of moving beyond the comforting belief that time and the generosity of its people will eventually solve America's racial problem.

I realize that even with the challenge to rethinking these stories pose, many people will find it difficult to embrace my assumption that racism is a permanent component of American life. Mesmerized by the racial equality syndrome, they are too easily reassured by simple admonitions to "stay on course," which come far too easily from those—black and white—who are not on the deprived end of the economic chasm between blacks and whites.

The goal of racial equality is, while comforting to many whites, more illusory than real for blacks. For too long, we have worked for substantive reform, then settled for weakly worded and poorly enforced legislation, indeterminate judicial decisions, token government positions, even holidays. I repeat. If we are to seek new goals for our struggles, we must first reassess the worth of the racial assumptions on which, without careful thought, we have presumed too much and relied on too long.

Let's begin.

CHAPTER 1

Racial Symbols: A Limited Legacy

So we stand here
On the edge of hell
In Harlem
And look out on the world
And wonder
What we're gonna do
In the face of
What we remember.

—Langston Hughes

"OH, THE CONTRADICTIONS OF CIVIL RIGHTS REPRESEN-tation," I said to no one in particular as, rushing from the site of one lecture in midtown Manhattan, I saw the car and driver waiting at the curb to drive me to a college in Westchester County, where I was to give another speech later that afternoon. Rather than a cab to the train and then another cab from train to campus, the lecture sponsors offered a car to convey me from door to door. I hesitated, not at the car's real convenience, but at the memory of the many times in the 1960s I'd flown—usually in first-class jets—to the South to represent poor black parents courageously trying to desegregate the public schools in their areas—usually at the risk of their jobs, or worse.

Now, getting in and settling myself in the roomy rear seat, I eased my guilt by determining to use the time to peruse the just-arrived manuscripts of Geneva Crenshaw's new stories. I noted with some satisfaction that my driver was black. In New York, as elsewhere, it has begun to seem that blacks, particularly black men, who lack at least two college degrees, are not hired in any position above the most menial.

As we got under way, I stifled a yawn. It had been a busy week. For far from the first time, I wondered why I accept lecture invitations while teaching full-time. The obvious reasons are the correct ones. I enjoy getting out my unorthodox views on racism, and the money—when I am paid—is always welcome. On this trip, I was scheduled to present my second of three lectures that week in connection with Martin Luther King, Jr.'s, birthday.

While hardly intended for that purpose, the national holiday on the third Monday in January to honor Dr. King serves as a two-week prelude to February's Black History Month. This six-week commemorative period is a boon to every black public figure—from politician to sports star—able to mount a platform and collect a fee. Black academics have certainly benefited in this speakers' market; and as a law teacher specializing in civil rights law, I receive many invitations during this annual interval of public interest in the problems of "our people."

Having convinced myself that the trip was valuable if not necessary, I decided to utilize the traveling time by reading one of Geneva's new stories. I was almost through the first when the driver braked hard to avoid a car that had cut into our lane. He apologized, and, nodding in response, I glanced at the driver's name tag and exclaimed aloud, "I don't believe it!"

"Don't believe what, brother?" the driver responded, turning slightly to face me. He was dark-skinned, thin, and probably in his late fifties.

"That your name is Jesse B. Semple."

"You may not believe it," he said, with an edge in his voice, "but that's been my name all my life, and I'm not about to change it."

"As you probably know," I replied, ignoring his annoyance, "that's quite a famous name. Langston Hughes regaled millions of black people over many years with his short essays about conversations with a street-wise Harlem black named Jesse B. Semple. Langston always called him Simple, and published, I think, five or six books of the Simple stories."*

---

* In a foreword to a collection of these stories, Langston Hughes wrote that Simple and the other characters in them were a composite of people he knew in Harlem. Simple first appeared in Hughes's columns in the *Chicago Defender* and the *New York Post* and, from 1950 on, in book form.[1] The *Encyclopaedia Britannica* describes Simple as a "hard-working, uneducated, but knowledgeable harlemite, . . . one of the master comic creations of the latter 20th century."[2]

"Who you telling?" the driver interjected, with obvious pride. He might, I thought, be no less proud of his driving, as effortlessly he maneuvered the large car through traffic as we headed up Central Park West.

"My mother loved Langston Hughes. Our family name was Semple, and it was a natural to name me Jesse B. If you know the character, you also know why I'm sure not sorry about the name."

"Simple certainly has plenty of mother wit and street smarts," I agreed.

"I've read all the Langston Hughes books," Semple said, "but that was years ago. Nowadays I'm too busy trying to make ends meet, though I still do some reading while I wait for clients."

"Things are tough for black folks these days," I remarked. "Still, quite a few black people feel we've come a long way, including even a national holiday in honor of Dr. Martin Luther King."

"Don't count me in that number!" Semple was vehement. "I hate to say it, but I worked my behind off gathering petitions. And for what? I think all but a few states have now joined the rest of the country in declaring a holiday celebrating Dr. King's birthday. Back then, I didn't think we could do it. And I was amazed when we did."*

---

* In 1986, after years of effort, and a last-ditch attempt by North Carolina's Republican Senator Jesse Helms to derail Senate action by calling for hearings on King's "action-oriented Marxism," the Senate (by a vote of 78 to 22) supported earlier House action to create the nation's tenth official holiday, in recognition of the civil rights contributions of Dr. Martin Luther King, Jr. President Reagan, who earlier had opposed the measure, promised to sign it. The holiday, commemorating the birth of Dr. King on 15 January 1929, is the third Monday in January.[3]

"And today?" I asked, surprised and pleased to see such 1960s-style militancy in a working-class black man with graying hair.

"Today I am older and wiser. A holiday for Dr. King is just another instance—like integration—that black folks work for and white folks grant when they realize—long before we do—that it is mostly a symbol that won't cost them much and will keep us blacks pacified. It's an updated version of the glass trinkets and combs they used in Africa a few centuries ago to trick some tribes into selling off their brothers and sisters captured from neighboring tribes."

"Likely," I said in their defense, "the tribes doing the selling thought they were getting something of great value."

"They did, and they were," Semple responded. "They were getting symbols of the white man's power. They saw the power he had to travel the seas in his large ships, and they wanted some of that power. They saw the power he had to kill from a great distance, and they wanted some of *that* power. Those Africans thought those trinkets were symbols of white power. They were, but they were symbols, not of ships and guns, but of white mendacity, white deceit, white chicanery. And that is just what we are still asking for and what, after a big struggle, we are still getting!"

"I understand how you feel, Mr. Semple. Your bitterness mirrors my own when I think about all the school systems I helped desegregate back in the 1960s, sure that I was guaranteeing thousands of black children a quality, desegregated education. It took me a long time to recognize that school officials—when they finally complied with desegregation court orders—were creating separate educational programs for black children within schools that were integrated in name only. In fact, they were too often resegregated by 'ability groups,' denied black teachers and administrators, disproportionately disciplined for the least infractions deemed threatening to whites, and generally made to feel like aliens in what were supposed to be their schools.

"But," I added, "you shouldn't be too hard on yourself and others. The country has only a few national holidays celebrating the birthdays of its greatest heroes. I give credit to the persistence of thousands of people—including Coretta King, Democratic Congressman John Conyers of Detroit, and the entertainer Stevie Wonder—whose dedicated work made Dr. King's birthday one of them. Things are tough for black folks, Mr. Semple, but they don't get any better by ignoring the few positive spots on an otherwise bleak horizon. As the old folks used to say," I added expansively, "'black folks use to not have show, but we sho got show now.'"

"You wrong, man," Semple said disgustedly. "All most of us got is symbols." He paused to ensure that I got his point, and, when I didn't disagree, continued. "From the Emancipation Proclamation on, the Man been handing us a bunch of bogus freedom checks he never intends to honor. He makes you work, plead, and pray for them, and then when he has you either groveling or threatening to tear his damn head off, he lets you have them as though they were some kind of special gift. As a matter of fact, regardless of how great the need is, he only gives *you* when it will do *him* the most good!

"And before you can cash them in," Semple said heatedly, "the Man has called the bank and stopped payment or otherwise made them useless—except, of course, as symbols.

"You know Langston Hughes, man"—and his voice took on a lecturing note—"but you need to read your black history. Get into some John Hope Franklin, Vincent Harding, Mary Berry, and Nathan Huggins. Or, if you don't believe black historians, try Eugene Genovese, Leon Litwack, and C. Vann Woodward. They will all tell you that is how it has been, and that is how it is now."

I was delighted. Semple was right on target. "I do read," I assured him, "and I agree with your assessment of racial symbols. The fact is, though, that most whites and lots of black folks rely on symbols to support their belief that black people have come a long way since slavery and segregation to the present time. In their view, we not only have laws protecting our rights, but a holiday recognizing one of our greatest leaders."

"They all dreamers, man," Semple interrupted. "And stupid dreamers at that. I tell you those are the same fools who urged the Senate to confirm Clarence Thomas to the Supreme Court all during the summer of 'ninety-one, despite his anti–civil rights record, despite the fact he was put up there by the right wing's top men."

Semple, seeing traffic blocked ahead by a large truck, smoothly backed out of the crosstown street and proceeded up the avenue. Although it was an intricate maneuver involving forcing a few cars behind him to give way, he managed without interrupting his train of thought.

"That appointment was a mockery of Justice Thurgood Marshall's service to blacks. I saw that right away. I only regret I didn't see a holiday for Dr. King would mostly give a lot of token black government types, civil rights types, and scholar types a reason to bore us working-class folks to death with their speeches about what a great life Dr. King lived, with not near enough mention of how he died. Which, as I assume you know, is how Malcolm X died, and Medgar Evers,* and God knows how many other blacks who were killed because they had the gumption to tell the truth about the conditions blacks live in in this country, and then got down off the speaker's stand and actually tried to do something to improve them."

I nodded thoughtfully, making a mental note not to mention the purpose of my Westchester trip. All the way back to Nat Turner, black leaders—including Marcus Garvey, Paul Robeson, and W. E. B. Du Bois—have been killed or pushed out of the country because they posed a threat to white people.

While I was musing, Semple continued to preach, his voice louder, his tone more strident. "What you have is a holiday for one black man, great as he was, while the country does nothing about the fact that there are more black people out of work now than at any time since slavery. Tell me what's to celebrate about the condition of black people who die too soon, go to prison too long, and come to know life's blues far too early? Tell me how a holiday for Dr. King helps the poor, the ignorant, the out-of-work, and hungry blacks all over this racist land?"

I recognized that Semple was speaking as much out of his experience as out of the books he read. He sounded like the working-class men in black barbershops who may have

---

* Medgar Evers, leader of the Mississippi branch of the NAACP, was shot in the back and killed outside his home in June 1963.[4]

to keep quiet not to lose their jobs, but in their environment, talking to their friends, let it all come out. Far from being so beaten down making a living as to have stopped caring about their race, their rhetoric makes it seem as if the revolution is not simply imminent but already under way.

"I'm glad to see you're a race man," I told Semple, "but don't be so negative. We have to be ready for the long haul. I know, as Langston Hughes wrote in a poem, that life for blacks ain't been no crystal stair.[5] But we need some victories to keep our spirits up, and the King holiday *is* a victory, however grudgingly acknowledged by President Reagan, who claimed initially that it was neither necessary nor justified. As the old folks would put it, 'We ain't what we going to be, but thank God, we ain't what we was.'"

"That's wrong, man. Look!" Semple explained quietly and deadly serious. "You are a brother able to afford a limo for a trip to Westchester that most people make by train, you carry your clothes in Hartmann luggage, and you dress like you are related to the Brooks Brothers—but you need to get off quoting the old folks and open your eyes to what is going down right around you in the here and now."

"I think, Mr. Semple, that I am aware——"

"Aware don't make it, man! You got to be *with* it, like the rappers.[6] I bet you don't even listen to their music unless one of the groups gets tossed in jail for bodacious language. But read what John Edgar Wideman says about them. He makes my point."

Handing me one of a pile of books on the floor beside him, Semple stopped talking and concentrated on driving

across 125th Street—a detour required by a massive traffic
jam on the West Side Drive. I read quickly the heavily under-
lined passages their author, the novelist John Wideman, had
written about rappers:

> Like angry ancestral spirits, the imperatives of tradition
> rose up, reanimated themselves, mounted the corner chant-
> ers and hip hoppers. As soul diminished to a category on
> the pop charts, the beat from the street said no-no-no,
> you're too sweet. Try some of this instead. Stomp your
> feet. . . . Hit it. Hit. Boom. Crank up the volume. Bare
> bones percussion and chant holler scream. Our loud selves,
> our angry selves . . . sounds of city, of machines of inner
> space and outer space merge. Boom boxes. Doom boxes.
> Call the roll of the ancestors. . . .
>
> Rap burst forth precisely where it did, when it did be-
> cause that's where the long, long night of poverty and
> discrimination, of violent marginality remained a hurting
> truth nobody else was telling. That's where the creative en-
> ergies of a subject people were being choked and channeled
> into self-destruction.[7]

Glancing out the car window, I saw much more evidence
on Harlem's main thoroughfare than I needed of the points
both Wideman and Semple were making. Semple was more
correct than he perhaps realized. He intuitively understood
black history and the role of racism in this country as well as
many scholars who have studied it for years. I wondered: if
he'd gotten the breaks I had, gone to school, gained the jobs

degrees open up, which of us would be riding, and which driving the limo? It is the same thought I have when I speak with groups of black men in prison, their often impressive intelligence lost in frustration and bitterness. Born into a system in which they have never had a chance, they are reduced to one or another variant of what even they would agree is "shucking and jiving."

Still, symbols have been the mainstay of blacks' faith that some day they will truly be free in this land of freedom. Not just holidays, but most of our civil rights statutes and court decisions have been more symbol than enforceable law. We hail and celebrate each of these laws, but none of them is, as Semple put it, fully honored at the bank.

"It ain't pretty out there," he observed, catching my eye. "And now that we got a black mayor, one more symbol, the white folks will blame us if we don't clean up a mess they been making for decades."

"Mayor David Dinkins is doing what he can," I replied. "But however worthwhile their election, African Americans in public office, including the mayors of several major cities, lack the resources to address the problems they inherit, and thus can do little to overcome either unemployment or poverty. Black mayors are, nevertheless, expected to control black crime, particularly that affecting whites. When racial tensions erupt into incidents of random and organized violence, elected black representatives are expected—as their first priority—to keep the peace."

"You got that right, brother!" Semple laughed. "We black folks get into mayors' jobs the way we get into all-white neighborhoods—when the housing stock is run down, maintenance is expensive, and past abuse and mismanagement by whites make it impossible for blacks to do anything. Of course, despite horrendous social problems, eroded tax bases, departed businesses, and dispirited civil servants, the black mayors are blamed for disasters that were bound to happen given the way the whites ran the city at a time when black people had no control."

The car negotiated the traffic of the East Harlem streets. The obviously Spanish neighborhoods seemed to have a vitality lacking in the black ghetto. I wondered, not for the first time, whether even these non-English-speaking immigrants would make it in America while poor blacks or their survivors remain steeped in misery.

"You're right," I said, breaking the silence. "It is pretty depressing, Mr. Semple."

"It is and it ain't," he replied thoughtfully. Free of the city traffic, the car was making good time up the Major Deegan Expressway. The more open vistas seem to lighten Semple's thoughts. "Fact is," he said, "given the burdens our people are carrying, it's a wonder they're not all strung out on drugs or otherwise destroying themselves. The fact is, most people in those neighborhoods we drove through, tryin' to live decent, and they do it in part by living on symbols. Religious symbols, freedom symbols, legal symbols, and now holiday symbols. They are all but worthless at the bank, but sometimes black folks don't try to cash them there. Know what I mean?"

"I think so," I replied. "You know the Emancipation Proclamation as a legal matter freed no slaves. It exempted slave owners in Northern territory and, of course, had no effect on those in Confederate areas. But it was a potent symbol for the slaves, many of whom simply took off when they learned that Lincoln had issued a freedom order."

"That's something I didn't know," Semple said. "I do remember, though, that it was black folks who gave meaning to the Supreme Court's school desegregation decision of 1954. It promised a lot, but gave us 'all deliberate speed,'[8] which would have translated into not a damned thing if Dr. King in Montgomery, the freedom riders in Birmingham and Jackson, and those college students in North Carolina had not proved to us that segregation would not work if black folks didn't go along with it."

"Professor Patricia Williams would sum up our discussion about black folks and symbols as rights.[9] She agrees with you that blacks have little reason to expect constitutional rights will be fully enforced, and says:

> [I]t is also true that blacks always believed in rights in some larger, mythological sense—as a pantheon of possibility. It is in this sense that blacks believed in rights so much and so hard that we gave them life where there was none before; held onto them, put the hope of them into our wombs, mothered them, not the notion of them; we nurtured rights and gave rights life. And this was not the dry process of reification, from which life is drained and reality fades as the cement of conceptual determinism hardens round, but its opposite. This was the story of Phoenix; the parthenogenesis of unfertilized hope.[10]

"Strong words," Semple agreed. "I'm glad she's a law teacher."

"Why's that?"

"Maybe she can get beyond so many of our bourgeoisie black folks with all their degrees and fancy titles who still don't understand what we ordinary black folks have known for a very long time."

"Which is?" I asked rather defensively.

"Which is that the law works for the Man most of the time, and only works for us in the short run as a way of working for him in the long run."

I had to laugh in spite of myself. Semple was a marvel. "You will be happy to know," I told him, "that some middle-class black professionals agree with you. Plus, Mr. Semple," I admonished, "you are too hard on those of us who managed to get degrees and what you call a bourgeois life style. I have to tell you that neither offers real protection from racial discrimination. We are both black—and, for precisely that reason, we are in the same boat."

"Not really, brother," Semple said. "I mean no offense, but the fact is you movin'-on-up black folks hurt us everyday blacks simply by being successful. The white folks see you doing your thing, making money in the high five figures, latching on to all kinds of fancy titles, some of which even have a little authority behind the name, and generally moving on up. They conclude right off that discrimination is over, and that if the rest of us got up off our dead asses, dropped the welfare tit, stopped having illegitimate babies, and found jobs, we would all be just like you.

"It's not fair, brother, but it's the living truth. You may be committed to black people but, believe me, you have to work very hard to do as much *good* for black people as you do harm simply by being good at whatever you do for a living!"

"That's a pretty heavy burden to hang on anybody," I suggested, "though I often make the same point in my lectures. I assume," I added, "that you don't include Dr. King in your condemnation."

"Man, get it straight," Semple replied. "I don't include anyone! It's the white folks who make these conclusions. We black folks, working-class and upper-class, simply have to live with them.

"But," he continued, his voice softening, "you're right. Dr. King was recruited by the masses back in Montgomery and responded to the call with some down-home, black Baptist leadership for us and some pretty potent philosophy for the rest of you. Even so, I don't think middle-class blacks and many liberal whites really accepted King until 1964 when he received the Nobel Peace Prize."

"And," I interjected, "many blacks and liberals were appalled when he spoke out early against the war in Vietnam and then shifted his campaign from race to poverty."

"Folks got one-track minds," Semple explained. "It's like with Jesse Jackson. He was O.K. as a quick-mouth preacher with his Operation PUSH* telling ghetto kids to stop listening

---

* PUSH is the acronym for People United to Save Humanity, an organization founded by Jackson in the wake of Martin Luther King, Jr.'s, assassination in 1968.

to those 'Do It to Me Baby' lyrics on those so-called soul radio stations. He was O.K. when he had them repeat 'I Am Somebody,' in the outside hope that a few of them might believe it despite the whole world telling them that they are, have been, and will be—nothing. But when Jackson decides to run for president, suddenly he is a joke. I am still hoping to laugh with him right into the White House."

"I supported Reverend Jackson in both 1984 and 1988," I commented, "but given your views about white people, don't you have to agree that we will have to wait for a more mainstream black politician who has a realistic shot of some day reaching the White House?"

Semple half turned so as to see me while keeping one eye on the highway. "Man, I don't read tea leaves, or in other ways foretell the future, but if Jesse Jackson ever decided to run again, he has my vote locked up. He is my kind of black man. Over the years, Jesse has given me plenty of reason for pride in him and in me. Sure, he has made some mistakes—and white folks won't let him forget them. But he has done some things, taken positions, achieved some political gains that in spiritual terms were worth a million dollars to me, as broke as I am. And that's the kind of money on which I pay no taxes, and it keeps on earning interest even though I do not take it near a bank—or a bar. If you get my point."

"I guess we both agree Jackson is an important symbol for black people."

"A *very* important one. Thing is," Semple added, "I don't want my symbols on the shelf. I want them in action, embarrassing white folks and mobilizing black folks to take themselves seriously. So I hope Jackson will run for president again, if not in 'ninety-two, at least in 'ninety-six. He may never win, but that's like saying we may never get free. Nothing going to happen unless we keep trying. And with Jackson still active, we can expect some more Michael Jordan–type moves, political slam-dunks in which he does the impossible and looks good while doing it."

I liked Semple's basketball imagery. "Jackson's as much a marvel at the podium as Jordan is on the basketball court. Problem is," I mused, "too many whites can't get past Jackson's color to hear his message. That's why this country needs a white Jesse Jackson—the political equivalent of these white pop singers who, even as poor facsimiles of black entertainers, become stars earning big bucks because the white public is able to identify with them."

"I know what you mean, brother," Semple responded, "but a white Jesse Jackson is like a white Michael Jordan."

"Meaning?" I asked, smiling at Semple's not-so-subtle racial chauvinism.

"Meaning that Jesse not only got a soulful preaching style. He also got the nerve to be different, be his own person. In short, man, he got the courage to fail. When you find a white person with those qualities, I will listen to him or her. And so, I would hope, will white people."

"Are you suggesting that until white folks get smart, black folks will never be free?"

"I don't ever see white people getting smart about race," Semple said seriously. "Unless there is a crisis, they learn nothing! And if they can get out of a bad situation by messing with our rights, that is what they do, have been doing for two hundred years, and likely will continue to do."

Semple turned into the college's main gates. As we headed toward the administration building where he was to drop me off, I thanked Semple for the ride. "It was good talking to you. You know," I remarked, "you need to share your survival secret. How do you keep all that anger aimed at whites when so many black men turn it on their families, each other, themselves?"

"I ain't no saint, man. My rage is big enough to hurt family, friends, *and* myself—and still have plenty left over. Only thing is I still remember the root cause of my anger." He paused, thinking. "Guess I don't have no secret, but I think my philosophy—if that's what it is—is in Toni Morrison's novel *Beloved*. Remember, the character Denver is terrified of white people, and with good reason. In slavery, they'd whipped her mother while she was pregnant, and crippled her grandma, jailed her mother, owned everything.

"All of these memories scared her to death, and Denver has not left her house for years. But now, needing to get help for her sick mother, she stands on the porch trying to get up courage to leave, and has this imaginary conversation with her grandma, an escaped slave who had told her about how evil whites can be.

"'But you said there was no defense,' Denver says, meaning against white people," Semple explained.

"'There ain't,' says her grandma in her mind.

"'Then what do I do?'

"'Know it, and go on out the yard. Go on.'"[11]

"That is not only a good philosophy," I told Semple, "but it may be the only philosophy that makes sense for blacks in this country."

Semple shook his head. "Maybe," he said, "but old as I'm gettin', sometimes I want to go the advice Denver got one better and just keep going right on out of this racist land."

"Emigrate, you mean?" I asked. "While there is a rich and mostly untold history of blacks moving to escape racial persecution and gain a better life, do you think it offers an answer to our current problems? Certainly, not many of my students do."

"That's because most of your students are privileged. Some of your black ones probably wouldn't recognize racism unless it rose up and bit them—as it probably will at some point! And the white ones really think racism is over, despite anything we tell them."

"Still," I replied, "giving up all you have here is a pretty drastic solution."

"People looking to escape are not worried about solutions," Semple said. "They just want to get away. Let me put it this way. Every year or so, my wife and I take off for a week or so to one of the Caribbean islands. My wife has family living in Barbados, but we've been to several islands. There, we see black people—people who look like us—doing everything, running things, managing them, owning them. I feel proud and envious—even though those people are as exploited as we are back here. Being there, it's easy to imagine ourselves part of a black-run society, and it just makes us feel good."

"A black Camelot is not necessarily what you'd get," I warned. "Look at Haiti and any number of African countries."

"I know all that," Semple conceded. "Still, a homeland, even a place I can never go to, makes me feel better about who I am and where I am. We were talkin' about symbols. Well, most whites have a homeland that gives them feelings of pride though their families left there generations ago— with no intention to return. If whites need that kind of symbol, you know we need it. Guess a homeland for America's black folks, well, that's the biggest symbol of all. Always has been for us. You have any doubt, you listen to the words of that spiritual 'City Called Heaven.' Know it?"

I confessed that I hadn't heard it in years and had forgotten the words.

"Don't forget your roots, brother," Semple admonished me as he reached the administration building, where a group of people were waiting on the steps. His window was open, and I could see their faces registering a mixture of bafflement and pleasure as Semple's rich tenor, reminiscent of Roland Hayes's, reached them:

> *I am a poor pilgrim of sorrow,*
> *I'm tossed in this wide world alone,*
> *No hope have I for tomorrow,*
> *I've started to make heav'n my home.*[12]

CHAPTER 2

The Afrolantica Awakening

[T]he idea of a black nation seems so farfetched as
to be ludicrous, but if you entertain it for a minute,
even as an impossible dream, it should give you a
feeling of wholeness and belonging you've never
had and can never have as long as blacks have to
live in a country where they are despised.

—Julius Lester

THE FIRST OCEANOGRAPHERS TO REPORT UNUSUAL RUM-
blings in the middle of the Atlantic Ocean, some nine
hundred miles due east of South Carolina, speculated that
some sort of land mass was rising up from the ocean bottom.
Naturally, these reports were dismissed as the work of crazies
or, worse, of publicity-seeking scientists. Even more outrageous seemed these scientists' further hypothesis that this land
mass was the fabled Atlantis—a body of land the ancients accepted as real, Plato describing it as the "lost continent of

Atlantis."[1]* But gradually people began to take seriously the message of the insistent churning that made a hundred-mile area of the ocean impossible for even the most powerful ships to navigate. Night after night for several months, Americans sat glued to their television screens to watch the underwater camera pictures of a huge mass rising slowly out of the ocean depths. Then, one evening, a vast body of land roared into view like an erupting volcano.

For several weeks, the area was cloaked in boiling-hot steam and impenetrable mist. When the air finally cleared, observers in high-flying planes saw a new land, complete with tall mountains that sheltered fertile valleys and rich plains already lush with vegetation. The new Atlantis was surrounded by beautiful beaches punctuated by deep-water harbors. From all indications, the land—roughly the size of the New England states—was uninhabited, though from afar you could see that fish filled its streams and animals in great abundance roamed its fields. Less picturesque but of more interest to potential developers, scientific tests performed from planes and space satellites suggested that the earth on this Atlantis contained substantial deposits of precious minerals, including gold and silver.

The United States and several other countries wasted no time in dispatching delegations to claim the land or portions of it. Several skirmishes by well-armed expeditions indicated that major nations would bitterly contest ownership of the

---

* It was variously spelled Atlantis, Atalantica, or Atalantis; the legend of its existence and its strange disappearance persisted through the Middle Ages and even after the Renaissance.

new Atlantis. Nature, however, proved a more serious barrier to occupying the new land than did greed-motivated combat.

The first explorers, an American force escorted by a heavily armed battle crew, landed by helicopter. They barely escaped with their lives. The crew members had a hard time breathing and managed to take off just as they were beginning to lose consciousness. The experience was sufficiently painful and scary that none of those who came out of it wanted to try a second time. Subsequent efforts by the United States, other major nations, and independent adventurers to land either by air or by water also failed, even though the landing parties were equipped with space suits and breathing equipment that had sustained human life on the moon or hundreds of feet under the sea. On the new continent, the air pressure—estimated at twice the levels existing at the bottom of the sea—threatened human life. One survivor explained that it was like trying to breathe under the burdens of all the world—a description that was to take on a special social significance not initially apparent.

What frustration! This exciting new land mass seemed to be aching for exploration and, of course, development. Ceasing their competition, the major powers cooperated in one enormously expensive effort after another, all intended to gain access to Atlantis. All failed. Not even the world's most advanced technology allowed human beings to survive on those strange shores, so inviting seen from afar; and they proved totally inhospitable to a series of approaches.

Then a team of four U.S. Navy divers tried to reach the new land under water. A submarine entered a deep harbor and emitted the divers through a special chamber. They swam underwater through the harbor and into the mouth of a large river. All seemed to go well until, a few hundred yards up the river, the divers suddenly began to experience the breathing difficulties that had thwarted earlier explorers. Turning immediately, they started back to the submarine; but they had gone too far and, long before reaching the harbor, began to lose consciousness.

The crew chief, Ensign Martin Shufford, managed to link the three groggy team members together with a slender cable and to tow them back to the submarine. When the divers revived, they hailed Shufford as a hero. He declined the honor, insisting that he had not had trouble breathing—that, in fact, he'd felt really invigorated by the new land's waters. And a medical check found him normal. The only difference between Shufford and the members of his crew (and, indeed, all those who had tried previously to land on Atlantis) was race. Martin Shufford was an American black man.

Initially, neither the military nor government officials viewed this fact as significant. After all, peoples of color from other countries, including Africa, had tried to land on the new land with the usual near-fatal results. Even so, there was no denying the evidence of the Martin Shufford rescue. African Americans did appear immune to the strange air pressures that rendered impossible other human life on the new Atlantis.

In an effort to determine whether other African Americans could survive on Atlantis—a possibility many believed, given the new land's importance, highly inappropriate—the next helicopter expedition carried on board three African-American men and, as pilot, an African-American woman. An amazed world watched the landing, filmed by a crew member and beamed back via satellite for televising. After a cautious first few steps, the crew discovered that they needed neither their space suits nor special breathing equipment. In fact, the party felt exhilarated and euphoric—feelings they explained upon their reluctant return (in defiance of orders, they spent several days exploring the new land) as unlike any alcohol- or drug-induced sensations of escape. Rather, it was an invigorating experience of heightened self-esteem, of liberation, of waking up. All four agreed that, while exploring what the media were now referring to as "Afrolantica," they felt *free*.

Cautiously, blacks began wondering whether Afrolantica might not be their promised land. Incredulity changed to excitement as more and more African Americans visited it and found it both habitable and inviting. Many people drew a parallel with the Hebrews' experiences in the Book of Exodus (13:21), as did one black minister in an oft-quoted sermon after a trip to Afrolantica:

> For the Israelites of old, the Lord made Himself into a pillar of cloud by day and a pillar of fire by night to lead them to the light. Are we less needy than were they? We, like them, have wandered in a hostile wilderness for not forty but closer to four hundred years. We, like them, have suffered the destruction of slavery—and, in addition, the second-class status of segregation. Now we endure the hateful hypocrisy of the equal-opportunity era that, like the "separate but equal" standard it replaced, denies the very

opportunity its name proclaims. But at long last the Lord has sent us a home that is as hostile to others as America has been to us. Let us go there and show what—given the chance—we might have done *here!*

Many, but far from all, African Americans shared this minister's enthusiasm. A spokeswoman for the opposition, having successfully demanded equal TV time, explained: "Emigrating to Afrolantica would be to abandon a civilization we have helped create for a wilderness that could prove an enticing trap. Life in America is hard for African Americans," she acknowledged, "but, my friends, be warned. For us, the Exodus story is both inaccurate as analogy and frightening as prediction.

First, it is inaccurate as a measure of our present condition: we are not slaves to any pharaoh. Second, the forty years the Israelites wandered in the wilderness after leaving Egypt was a dire experience few of us would view as an acceptable substitute for life in America. We must not surrender the gains made through our civil rights efforts. We must not relinquish the labor of the generations who came before us and for whom life was even harder than it is for us. America, whether whites like it or not, is our land, too. We would like to visit Afrolantica, but our home is here.

A pro-emigration group introduced legislation in Congress that would provide twenty thousand dollars to each African-American citizen wishing to emigrate to Afrolantica. This "Reparations Subsidy" would finance the move and was to be repaid if a recipient sought to return in less than ten years. Emigration opponents attacked the legislation as both bad policy and unconstitutional because it created and offered benefits based on a recipient's race without citing a compelling state interest to justify a suspect racial classification.[2] This legislation—though never enacted—sparked a debate on Afrolantica which pre-empted all other civil rights issues in households across America.

Each side found support for its arguments in the nearly two hundred years of efforts—led by whites as well as blacks—to establish a homeland on the continent of Africa where slaves or ex-slaves might go or be sent.[3] Both sides were as divided over the issue as were their forebears, though both acknowledged that whites had, from the beginning, fostered efforts at black emigration in an "endless cycle" of pushing blacks around in accordance with the political and economic needs of the moment.

Supporters of Afrolantican emigration took as their models three key advocates of emigration between the early nineteenth century and the 1920s: Paul Cuffe, Martin R. Delany, and Marcus Garvey. The first, Paul Cuffe, was a black shipowner from Massachusetts who, himself a constant victim of persecution (he was jailed for his refusal to pay taxes, which he withheld to protest being denied the vote and other privileges of citizenship), had determined to "emancipate" Africa. Between 1811 and 1816, Cuffe had, at his own expense, led voyages of blacks to Sierra Leone (the British having already established a colony there for the purpose of resettling several hundred destitute and friendless blacks who had gone to England after fighting on its side in the Revolutionary War in return for their freedom).[4] The fact that Cuffe's movement had been curtailed by his death in 1817 scarcely dampened the enthusiasm of the blacks who wanted to emigrate to Afrolantica. Indeed, it merely heightened their enthusiasm to revive the memory of this early black hero.

Later, in the mid-1850s, the black leader, physician, and journalist Martin R. Delany had—in line with the preference of contemporary black leaders for Central America or Haiti over Africa as a place for black resettlement—arranged for two thousand black people to sail to Haiti.[5] But the most potent of these great advocates of black emigration was certainly Marcus Garvey.[6] In the 1920s, this charismatic Jamaican immigrant had founded the Universal Negro Improvement Association, which managed to raise, in only a few years, ten million dollars and attracted at least half a million members. Although Garvey made definite plans for emigration to Africa, buying and equipping ships, they were frustrated when—in a highly controversial case—he was convicted of using the mails to defraud and sentenced to five years in prison, fined one thousand dollars, and required to pay court costs. Though pardoned by President Calvin Coolidge in 1927, he was deported as an undesirable alien; and his subsequent efforts to revive his movement failed. The blacks who wanted to emigrate to Afrolantica pointed out that all these earlier advocates of emigration had themselves been driven to take their stand by their experience of slavery or segregation and by their perception that the discrimination, exclusion, and hostility from whites was never going to end. Garvey himself had told blacks that racial prejudice was so much a part of the white civilization that it was futile to appeal to any sense of justice or high-sounding democratic principles.*

On the other side, American blacks opposing Afrolantican emigration pointed out that, while some blacks had indeed been interested in emigration over the last two centuries, relatively few had actually left America.[8] Moreover, the initial impetus had come from whites, who had by the 1830s managed to place some fourteen hundred blacks in Liberia. Then the movement lost steam, though it was endorsed in the 1850s by the Republican party and some abolitionists supported it. These anti-Afrolantica blacks maintained that African Americans must not give up their long equality struggle: after all, it had transformed the Constitution from being a document primarily protective of both property and its owners, to one aimed to protect individual rights—and as such was a shield that, however flawed, was the envy of the free world. The slavery and segregation eras were important history, but they were just that—history. They were not cast

---

* From the Atlanta penitentiary, Garvey wrote his followers:

    My months of forcible removal from among you, being imprisoned as a punishment for advocating the cause of our real emancipation, have not left me hopeless or despondent; but to the contrary, I see a great ray of light and the bursting of a mighty political cloud which will bring you complete freedom. . . .

    We have gradually won our way back into the confidence of the God of Africa, and He shall speak with a voice of thunder, that shall shake the pillars of a corrupt and unjust world, and once more restore Ethiopia to her ancient glory.[7]

from some eternal, social mold determining all of America's racial policies.

The plight of the black underclass was still, of course, cause for the deepest concern, but government policies that favored the already well-off while ignoring the working class adversely affected whites as well as blacks. The debilitating burdens of poverty know no color line. The lessons of history could engender hope as well as deepen despair. And history suggested that if current trends of unemployment continued, the nation would soon have to consider legislation like that enacted during the Great Depression of the 1930s. These new laws would ease, if not eliminate, poverty, improve education, and guarantee employment opportunities for all. Having worked so hard to bring about these reforms, African Americans would be foolish to leave the American table just as the long-awaited banquet was about to be served.

In response, Afrolantica emigration advocates asked whether the banquet would be entirely devoid of racial discrimination. Or would America—"*our* country, after all," one of the leaders said—continue to demand that whites sit at the head of the table and be served first, leaving blacks at the foot with such dregs as they could scrape up?

Then these pro-emigration blacks moved forward their big gun: Abraham Lincoln. They noted the historian John Hope Franklin's comment that "Negro colonization seemed almost as important to Lincoln as emancipation. . . . Down to the end of the war Lincoln held out hope for colonizing at least some of the Negroes who were being set free."[9] In

an 1862 bill that sought to emancipate slaves in the District
of Columbia, Lincoln included a provision of one hundred
thousand dollars for the voluntary emigration, to Haiti and
Liberia, of former slaves; the bill was eventually enacted.
In the same year, he called a group of black leaders to the
White House and urged them to support colonization, stat-
ing: "Your race suffer greatly, many of them, by living among
us, while ours suffer from your presence. In a word we suffer
on each side. If this is admitted, it affords a reason why we
should be separated."[10]

Ready to rebut, blacks opposed to Afrolantica emigration cited Frederick Douglass, the most influential of the
black leaders of the time. He had always opposed emigration and, in November 1858, set out his position in his newspaper, *North Star*, with spine-tingling clarity:

We deem it a settled point that the destiny of the colored
man is bound up with that of the white people of this
country. . . . *We are here*, and here we are likely to be. To
imagine that we shall ever be eradicated is absurd and ri-
diculous. We can be remodified, changed, and assimilated,
but never extinguished. We repeat . . . that we are *here;* and
that this is *our* country; and the question for the philoso-
phers and statesmen of the land ought to be, what principles should dictate the policy of the action toward us? We
shall neither die out, nor be driven out; but shall go with
this people, either as a testimony against them, or as an
evidence in their favor throughout their generations. We
are clearly on their hands and must remain there forever.[11]

To counter this black patriotism, emigration advocates vehemently recalled the hopes so often dashed as, over the years, thousands of blacks had left their homes to seek elsewhere in America some better place, a place they could call their own, where they would not be harassed—or lynched; where they could live as the free citizens the government assured them they were.* But these efforts had been almost always met by opposition and further harassment.

Strongly promoting emigration to Afrolantica were black nationalist groups, who have traditionally made emigration or separation a major goal. They were especially attracted by the idea of an island of their own because their efforts to establish black communities in this country had been harshly opposed by whites, particularly law enforcement officials. For example, when in November 1969, white residents of St. Clair County, Alabama, learned that Black Muslims had purchased two large farms in the area, they organized a "Stop the Muslims" movement. Almost immediately Muslim members were subjected to criminal prosecution on various charges: trespass, "failure to register as a Muslim," acting as agent for an unlicensed foreign corporation, and "permitting livestock to run at large." Whites filed a civil suit for five hundred thousand dollars against the Muslims,

---

* Of course, while emigration efforts have not met with broad success, blacks have constantly immigrated from one portion of the country to another, seeking opportunity and acceptance. The escapes from slavery via the underground railroad brought countless blacks both to the North and to Canada. After the Civil War, scores of blacks headed west to Kansas, Texas, and California. There were major movements of black Americans from South to North during both world wars—all seeking employment, a better life, and racial equality.[12]

charging aggravated trespass and infringement upon use of land. The Muslims challenged these actions in a federal suit and obtained partial relief from a three-judge federal court.[13]

The court both invalidated the Alabama statute requiring registration of "communists, nazis, Muslims, and members of communist front organizations"; and halted the criminal prosecutions, except for the charge of "permitting livestock to run at large," finding that the Muslims had failed to show that this charge was used to discourage assertion of their First Amendment rights. The court also refused to enjoin the five-hundred-thousand-dollar damages action, though it acknowledged that the suit had a chilling effect on the plaintiffs' freedom of association rights. The Black Muslims later decided to sell their farm, after almost one third of their three hundred head of cattle had been poisoned or shot. The white man who had originally sold the land to the Muslims also suffered: his business was burned, acid was poured on his car, and his life was threatened. The Ku Klux Klan bought land surrounding the Muslim farm to "keep an eye on things." Thoroughly discouraged, the Muslims said they would sell their farm even to the Klan.[14]

Thus the debate raged on, as each side marshaled something out of history or experience to support its point of view. After some months, many outspoken blacks were quite ready to emigrate, but most were not. Whether ready to go or determined to stay, clearly all black people felt good about the opportunity. Blacks' enslaved forebears had, after learning of the Emancipation Proclamation, gained the courage to leave their masters' plantations. Now, the very idea of a continent emerged from the ocean and habitable only by black Americans awakened black pride—a term not much heard during the 1980s and 1990s. Self-esteem blossomed in the reflected glow of their Afrolantica option, and snuffed out both the manifest as well as the latent tendency toward self-deprecation that is unavoidably instilled in people sub-ordinated by outside forces.

While black people pondered, white Americans—contrary to their attitudes to black emigration in earlier decades—grew increasingly troubled by the blacks' new confidence: some whites thought it arrogant; others, "uppity"; all were unnerved by it. The linking of Afrolantica and freedom for African Americans, coming as new racial oppression swept the country in the mid-1990s, heightened racial tensions. Televised reports showing American blacks able to function normally on the rich new land sparked racial clashes and several attacks by white hoodlums on black communities. A man arrested at the scene of a race riot spoke for all hostile whites: "Damn! It ain't right! The niggers got sports and pop music all tied up. Now this! It's more than this God-fearing, America-loving white man can take!"

More sophisticated, though hardly less envious opinions were common in the press, in opinion polls, and on call-in talk shows. Black people were not surprised at the hostile reaction. "As with so much else," one black leader observed, "we are treated as aliens in our own country. Rather than view our ability to survive on the new land as a major victory for America, whites see it as a loss for them and a dangerous advantage for us."

Some conservatives feared Afrolantica could become another Cuba, insulated from American expansionism and, worse, beyond its power. Afrolantica, they warned, could serve as a rallying incentive for other third-world peoples who might conclude that white influence, rather than colored incompetence, was responsible for their poverty and powerlessness. Even without Afrolantica's insulating atmosphere, the long-subjugated colored peoples of Asia, Africa, and South America might rise up against the United States' tendency to subvert governments and exploit indigenous people and against its economic domination that has proven as oppressive as the political colonialism it replaced.

Before long, Afrolantica became a national obsession. Government officials hinted ominously about a dire plot to undermine world stability, economic security, and the American Way of Life. As a first defense, the government launched a quiet search for black leaders or academics who would support the conspiracy theory and condemn the emigration movement as subversive. Surprisingly, none could be found, though the undercover agents offered the usual rewards of money and prestige. In the past, such rewards had proven adequate to attract those members of the race all too ready to please whites regardless of the adverse consequences for blacks.

In the meantime, a large group of blacks decided to put an end to discussion and turned their energies to planning for emigration. In this they were inspired by the words of Bishop Henry M. Turner, the leader of a black emigration movement around the turn of the century: "We were born here, raised here, fought, bled and died here, and have a thousand times more right here than hundreds of thousands of those who help to snub, proscribe and persecute us, and that is one of the reasons I almost despise the land of my birth."[15] These blacks pooled their resources to obtain transportation and equipment needed to sustain life and build new communities in the new land. The Afrolantica emigration programs, like the Jewish movements to support Israel, gained the support of even blacks who did not wish to move there. The uniformity of this support served to heighten the fears of many whites that the new continent posed both a political and an economic threat. Together, government and corporate institutions erected innumerable barriers in the paths of blacks seeking to leave the country. Visas were not available, of course; and immigration officials warned that since Afrolantica did not exist as a governmental entity, blacks moving there might sacrifice both their citizenship and their entitlement to return to America—even to visit relatives and friends.

Soon these pro-emigration leaders found themselves facing an array of civil suits and criminal charges. Remembering how Marcus Garvey had been similarly hounded, blacks determined that his experience would not be repeated. They fought the anti-emigration policies with protests and boycotts. Unlike the Israelites of ancient Egypt before the first Passover, black people during this period did not rely on one leader or seek deliverance through one organization. Rather, they worked together in communities.

"There is," one black woman observed, "something of Moses within each of us that we must offer as a service, as a living sacrifice to those like ourselves."

And out of this miracle of cooperative effort was organized and implemented the Afrolantica Armada: a thousand ships of every size and description loaded with the first wave of several hundred thousand black settlers. It set out for Afrolantica early on one sunny Fourth of July morning.

They never made it. Within hours of their departure, they received weather reports of severe disturbances in the ocean around Afrolantica. The island that had stood for a year in clear sunlight, a beacon of hope to long-besieged blacks, was—for the first time since its emergence—enveloped in a thick mist. The emigrants pressed on, hoping they would not have to land in bad weather. Worrying also, because radar and sonar measurements strongly indicated that whatever process had raised the lost continent was reversing itself.

Then the mist rose. The sight that met the eyes of the blacks on the emigrant armada was amazing, terrifying. Afrolantica was sinking back into the ocean whence it had arisen. The blacks on the ships knew they were witnessing the greatest natural spectacle in world history. "My God, what's happening?" was the universal question. It was replaced almost immediately, in the minds of those who were watching from the safety of their television sets in America, by another: Was Afrolantica, after all, no more than a cruel hoax, Nature's seismic confirmation that African Americans are preordained to their victimized, outcast state?

But, to their surprise, the black men and women on board the armada felt neither grief nor despair as they watched the last tip of the great landmass slip beneath the waves, and the ocean spread sleek and clear as though Afrolantica had never been. They felt deep satisfaction—sober now, to be sure—in having gotten this far in their enterprise, in having accomplished it together. As the great ships swung around in the ocean to take them back to America, the miracle of Afrolantica was replaced by a greater miracle. Blacks discovered that they themselves actually possessed the qualities of liberation they had hoped to realize on their new homeland. Feeling this was, they all agreed, an Afrolantica Awakening, a liberation—not of place, but of mind.

One returning black settler spoke for all: "It was worth it just to *try* looking for something better, even if we didn't find it."

As the armada steamed back to America, people recalled the words of Frederick Douglass that opponents of emigration had cited to support their position: "We are Americans. We are not aliens. We are a component part of the nation. We have no disposition to renounce our nationality."[16] Even though they had rejected that argument, it had its truth. And it was possible to affirm it, and return to America, because they understood they need no longer act as the victims of centuries of oppression. They could act on their own, as their own people, as they had demonstrated to themselves and other blacks in their preparations to settle Afrolantica.

Their faces glowed with self-confidence, as they walked, erect and proud, down the gangplanks the next day when the ships returned to their home ports. The black men and women waiting to greet them, expecting to commiserate with them, were instead inspired. The spirit of cooperation that had engaged a few hundred thousand blacks spread to others, as they recalled the tenacity for humane life which had enabled generations of blacks to survive all efforts to dehumanize or obliterate them. Infectious, their renewed tenacity reinforced their sense of possessing themselves. Blacks held fast, like a talisman, the quiet conviction that Afrolantica had not been mere mirage—that somewhere in the word *America*, somewhere irrevocable and profound, there is as well the word *Afrolantica*.

CHAPTER 3

The Racial Preference Licensing Act

Racial nepotism rather than racial animus is the
major motivation for much of the discrimination
blacks experience.

—Matthew S. Goldberg

IT WAS ENACTED AS THE RACIAL PREFERENCE LICENSING
Act. At an elaborate, nationally televised signing ceremony,
the President—elected as a "racial moderate"—assured the
nation that the new statute represented a realistic advance
in race relations. "It is," he insisted, "certainly not a return
to the segregation policies granted constitutional protection
under the stigma-inflicting 'separate but equal' standard of
Plessy v. *Ferguson* established roughly a century ago.[1]

"Far from being a retreat into our unhappy racial past,"
he explained, "the new law embodies a daring attempt to

create a brighter racial future for all our citizens. Racial realism is the key to understanding this new law. It does not assume a nonexistent racial tolerance, but boldly proclaims its
commitment to racial justice through the working of a marketplace that recognizes and seeks to balance the rights of
our black citizens to fair treatment and the no less important
right of some whites to an unfettered choice of customers,
employees, and contractees."

Under the new act, all employers, proprietors of public facilities, and owners and managers of dwelling places, homes,
and apartments could, on application to the federal government, obtain a license authorizing the holders, their managers, agents, and employees to exclude or separate persons
on the basis of race and color. The license itself was expensive, though not prohibitively so. Once obtained, it required
payment to a government commission of a tax of 3 percent
of the income derived from whites employed, whites served,
or products sold to whites during each quarter in which a
policy of "racial preference" was in effect. Congress based
its authority for the act on the commerce clause, the taxing
power, and the general welfare clause of the Constitution.

License holders were required both to display their licenses prominently in a public place and to operate their
businesses in accordance with the racially selective policies
set out on their license. Specifically, discrimination had to
be practiced in accordance with the license on a nonselective
basis. Licenses were not available to those who, for example,
might hire or rent to one token black and then discriminate

against other applicants, using the license as a shield against discrimination suits. Persons of color wishing to charge discrimination against a facility not holding a license would carry the burden of proof, but such burden might be met with statistical and circumstantial as well as with direct evidence provided by white "testers."* Under the act, successful complainants would be entitled to damages set at ten thousand dollars per instance of unlicensed discrimination, including attorneys' fees.

License fees and commissions paid by license holders would be placed in an "equality fund" used to underwrite black businesses, to offer no-interest mortgage loans for black home buyers, and to provide scholarships for black students seeking college and vocational education. To counter charges that black people, as under *Plessy*, would be both segregated and never gain any significant benefit from the equality fund, the act provided that five major civil rights organizations (each named in the statute) would submit the name of a representative who would serve on the commission for one, nonrenewable three-year term.

---

* Testing is an effective, but too little utilized, technique to ferret out bias in the sale and rental of housing or in employment practices. Generally, in testing, people who are alike in virtually every way except race or ethnicity are sent to apply for jobs, housing, or mortgages. The results are then analyzed for how differently whites are treated compared with black or Hispanic people. In 1982, the Supreme Court found that testers in a housing discrimination suit, and the housing association to which they were attached, had standing to sue in their own right as injured parties.[2]

The President committed himself and his administration to the effective enforcement of the Racial Preference Licensing Act. "It is time," he declared, "to bring hard-headed realism rather than well-intentioned idealism to bear on our long-standing racial problems. Policies adopted because they seemed right have usually failed. Actions taken to promote justice for blacks have brought injustice to whites without appreciably improving the status or standards of living for blacks, particularly for those who most need the protection those actions were intended to provide.

"Within the memories of many of our citizens, this nation has both affirmed policies of racial segregation and advocated polices of racial integration. Neither approach has been either satisfactory or effective in furthering harmony and domestic tranquillity." Recalling the Civil Rights Act of 1964[3] and its 1991 amendments,[4] the President pointed out that while the once-controversial public-accommodation provisions in the original 1964 act received unanimous judicial approval in the year of its adoption,[5] even three decades later the act's protective function, particularly in the employment area, had been undermined by both unenthusiastic enforcement and judicial decisions construing its provisions ever more narrowly.

"As we all know," the President continued "the Supreme Court has now raised grave questions about the continued validity of the 1964 Act and the Fair Housing Act of 1968[6]—along with their various predecessors and supplemental amendments as applied to racial discrimination.

The Court stopped just short of declaring unconstitutional all laws prohibiting racial discrimination, and found that the existing civil rights acts were inconsistent with what it viewed as the essential 'racial forgiveness' principle in the landmark decision of *Brown* v. *Board of Education* of 1954.[7] The Court announced further that nothing in its decision was intended to affect the validity of the statutes' protection against discrimination based on sex, national origin, or religion.

"This is, of course, not an occasion for a legal seminar, but it is important that all citizens understand the background of the new racial preference statute we sign this evening. The Supreme Court expressed its concern that existing civil rights statutes created racial categories that failed to meet the heavy burden of justification placed on any governmental policy that seeks to classify persons on the basis of race. In 1989, the Court held that this heavy burden, called the 'strict scrutiny' standard, applied to remedial as well as to invidious racial classifications.[8] Our highest court reasoned that its 1954 decision in the landmark case of *Brown* v. *Board of Education* did not seek to identify and punish wrongdoers, and the implementation order in *Brown II*[9] a year later did not require immediate enforcement. Rather, *Brown II* asserted that delay was required, not only to permit time for the major changes required in Southern school policies, but also—and this is important—to enable accommodation to school integration which ran counter to the views and strong emotions of most Southern whites.

"In line with this reasoning," the President continued, "the Court referred with approval to the views of the late Yale law professor Alexander Bickel, who contended that any effort to enforce *Brown* as a criminal law would have failed, as have alcohol prohibition, antigambling, most sex laws, and other laws policing morals. Bickel said, 'It follows that in achieving integration, the task of the law . . . was not to punish law breakers but to diminish their number.'[10]

"Now the Court has found Professor Bickel's argument compelling. Viewed from the perspective provided by four decades, the Court says now that *Brown* was basically a call for a higher morality rather than a judicial decree authorizing Congress to coerce behavior allegedly unjust to blacks because that behavior recognized generally acknowledged differences in racial groups. This characterization of *Brown* explains why *Brown* was no more effective as an enforcement tool than were other 'morals-policing' laws such as alcohol prohibition, anti-gambling, and sex laws, all of which are hard to enforce precisely because they seek to protect our citizens' health and welfare against what a legislature deems self-abuse.

"Relying on this reasoning, the Court determined that laws requiring cessation of white conduct deemed harmful to blacks are hard to enforce because they seek to 'police morality.' While conceding both the states' and the federal government's broad powers to protect the health, safety, and welfare of its citizens, the Court found nothing in the Constitution authorizing regulation of what government at any particular time might deem appropriate 'moral' behavior. The exercise of such authority, the Court feared, could lead Congress to control the perceptions of what some whites believe about the humanity of some blacks. On this point," the President said, "I want to quote the opinion the Supreme Court has just handed down: 'Whatever the good intentions of such an undertaking, it clearly aimed for a spiritual result that might be urged by a religion but is beyond the reach of government coercion.'

"Many of us, of both political persuasions," the President went on, "were emboldened by the Court to seek racial harmony and justice along the route of mutual respect as suggested in its decision. This bill I now sign into law is the result of long debate and good-faith compromise. It is, as its opponents charge and its proponents concede, a radical new approach to the nation's continuing tensions over racial status. It maximizes freedom of racial choice for all our citizens while guaranteeing that people of color will benefit either directly from equal access or indirectly from the fruits of the license taxes paid by those who choose policies of racial exclusion.

"A few, final words. I respect the views of those who vigorously opposed this new law. And yet the course we take today was determined by many forces too powerful to ignore, too popular to resist, and too pregnant with potential to deny. We have vacillated long enough. We must move on toward what I predict will be a new and more candid and collaborative relationship among all our citizens. May God help us all as we seek with His help to pioneer a new path in our continuing crusade to bring justice and harmony to all races in America."

———

WELL, GENEVA, YOU'VE done it again, I thought to myself as I finished this second story well after midnight. After all our battles, I thought I'd finally pulled myself up to your advanced level of racial thinking—but the Racial Preference Licensing Act is too much.

"You still don't get it, do you?"

I looked up. There she was—the ultimate African queen—sitting on the small couch in my study. The mass of gray dreadlocks framing Geneva's strong features made a beautiful contrast with her smooth blue-black skin. She greeted me with her old smile, warm yet authoritative.

"Welcome," I said, trying to mask my shock with a bit of savoir-faire. "Do you always visit folks at two o'clock in the morning?"

She smiled. "I decided I could not leave it to you to figure out the real significance of my story."

"Well," I said, "I'm delighted to see you!" As indeed I was. It had been almost five years since Geneva disappeared at the close of the climactic civil rights conference that ended my book *And We Are Not Saved*. Seeing her now made me realize how much I had missed her, and I slipped back easily into our old relationship.

"Tell me, Geneva, how can you justify this law? After all, if the Fourteenth Amendment's equal protection clause retains any viability, it is to bar government-sponsored racial segregation. Even if—as is likely—you convince me of your law's potential, what are civil rights advocates going to say when I present it to them? As you know, it has taken me years to regain some acceptance within the civil rights community—since I suggested in print that civil rights lawyers who urge racial-balance remedies in all school desegregation cases were giving priority to their integration ideals over their clients' educational needs.[11] Much as I respect your insight on racial issues, Geneva, I think your story's going to turn the civil rights community against us at a time when our goal is to persuade them to broaden their thinking beyond traditional, integration-oriented goals."

"Oh ye of little faith!" she responded. "Even after all these years, you remain as suspicious of my truths as you are faithful to the civil rights ideals that events long ago rendered obsolete. Whatever its cost to relationships with your civil rights friends, accept the inevitability of my Racial Preference Licensing Act. And believe—if not me—yourself.

"Although you maintain your faith in the viability of the Fourteenth Amendment, in your writings you have acknowledged, albeit reluctantly, that whatever the civil rights law or constitutional provision, blacks gain little protection against one or another form of racial discrimination unless granting blacks a measure of relief will serve some interest of importance to whites.[12] Virtually every piece of civil rights legislation beginning with the Emancipation Proclamation supports your position.[13] Your beloved Fourteenth

Amendment is a key illustration of this white self-interest principle. Enacted in 1868 to provide citizenship to the former slaves and their offspring, support for the amendment reflected Republicans' concern after the Civil War that the Southern Democrats, having lost the war, might win the peace. This was not a groundless fear. If the Southern states could rejoin the union, bar blacks from voting, and regain control of state government, they might soon become the dominant power in the federal government as well.[14]

"Of course, within a decade, when Republican interests changed and the society grew weary of racial remedies and was ready to sacrifice black rights to political expediency, both the Supreme Court and the nation simply ignored the original stated purpose of the Fourteenth Amendment's equal protection guarantee. In 1896, the *Plessy* v. *Ferguson* precedent gave legal validity to this distortion and then to a torrent of Jim Crow statutes. 'Separate but equal' was the judicial promise. Racial subordination became the legally enforceable fact."

"Well, sure," I mustered a response, "the Fourteenth Amendment's history is a definitive example of white self-interest lawmaking, but what is its relevance to your Racial Preference Licensing Act? It seems to me—and certainly will seem to most civil rights advocates—like a new, more subtle, but hardly less pernicious 'separate but equal' law. Is there something I'm missing?"

"You are—which is precisely why I am here."

"I could certainly," I said, "use more of an explanation for a law that entrusts our rights to free-market forces. The law and economics experts might welcome civil rights protections in this form,* but virtually all civil rights professionals will view legalizing racist practices as nothing less than a particularly vicious means of setting the struggle for racial justice back a century. I doubt I could communicate them effectively to most black people."

"Of course you can't! Neither they nor you really want to come to grips with the real role of racism in this country."

"And that is?"

---

* These law and economics experts, especially Richard Posner and John J. Donohue, accept Gary Becker's theory that markets drive out discriminatory employers because discrimination tends to minimize profits.[15] The essence of Posner and Donohue's debate on Title VII (the Equal Employment Opportunity Act) is whether "[l]egislation that prohibits employment discrimination . . . actually enhance[s] rather than impair[s] economic efficiency."[16] Donohue argues that the effects of the Title VII statutory scheme are to increase the rate at which discriminators are driven out of the market from the base rate, which many economists steeped in the neoclassical tradition would argue is the optimal rate. Posner questions whether this effect (the increased rate) occurs; and, significantly, also raises questions about whether the regulatory scheme, designed to decrease discrimination against blacks in employment decisions and thereby increase the net welfare of blacks, actually succeeds in doing so. If neither assumption is accurate, he states that the costs of enforcement and all other costs associated with administering Title VII "are a dead weight social loss that cannot be justified on grounds [not only of efficiency but] of social equity."[17]

Posner and David A. Strauss both make statements that would seem to indicate openness to such measures as the Racial Preference Licensing Act. Posner writes that "it might be that a tax on those whites [who discriminate because of an aversion to blacks and therefore would seek a license] for the benefit of blacks would be justifiable on the grounds of social equity [although this is not an *efficiency* justification in the wealth maximization sense]."[18] And Strauss asks, "Why would the objectives of compensatory justice and avoiding racial stratification not be better served, at less cost, if the legal system permitted statistical discrimination; captured the efficiency gains (and the gains for reduced administrative costs) through taxation, and transferred the proceeds to African Americans?"[19]

"My friend, know it! Racism is more than a group of bad white folks whose discriminatory predilections can be controlled by well-formed laws, vigorously enforced. Traditional civil rights laws tend to be ineffective because they are built on a law enforcement model. They assume that most citizens will obey the law; and when law breakers are held liable, a strong warning goes out that will discourage violators and encourage compliance. But the law enforcement model for civil rights breaks down when a great number of whites are willing—because of convenience, habit, distaste, fear, or simple preference—to violate the law. It then becomes almost impossible to enforce, because so many whites, though not discriminating themselves, identify more easily with those who do than with their victims."

"That much I understand," I replied. "Managers of hotels, restaurants, and other places of public accommodation have complied with antidiscrimination laws because they have discovered that, for the most part, it is far more profitable to serve blacks than to exclude or segregate them. On the other hand, these same establishments regularly discriminate against blacks seeking jobs."

"Precisely right, friend. A single establishment, often a single individual, can be inconsistent for any number of reasons, including the desire not to upset or inconvenience white customers or white employees. More often, management would prefer to hire the white than the black applicant. As one economist has argued, 'racial nepotism' rather than 'racial animus' is the major motivation for much of the discrimination blacks experience."[20]

"But nepotism," I objected, "is a preference for family members or relatives. What does it have to do with racial discrimination?"

Geneva gave me her "you are not serious" smile.

Then it hit me. "Of course! You're right, Geneva, it is hard to get out of the law enforcement model. You're suggesting that whites tend to treat one another like family, at least when there's a choice between them and us. So that terms like 'merit' and 'best qualified' are infinitely manipulable if and when whites must explain why they reject blacks to hire 'relatives'—even when the only relationship is that of race. So, unless there's some pressing reason for hiring, renting to, or otherwise dealing with a black, many whites will prefer to hire, rent to, sell to, or otherwise deal with a white—including one less qualified by objective measures and certainly one who is by any measure better qualified."

"Lord, I knew the man could figure it out! He just needed my presence."

"Well, since a little sarcasm is the usual price of gaining face-to-face access to your insight, Geneva, I am willing to pay. Actually, as I think about it, racial licensing is like that approach adopted some years ago by environmentalists who felt that licensing undesirable conduct was the best means of dealing with industry's arguments that it could not immediately comply with laws to protect the environment. The idea is, as I recall, that a sufficiently high licensing fee would make it profitable for industry to take steps to control the emissions (or whatever), and that thereby it would be possible to reduce damage to health and property much more cheaply than an attempt to control the entire polluting activity.[21]*

"Come to think of it, Geneva, there's even a precedent, of sorts, for the Equality Fund. College football's Fiesta Bowl authorities no doubt had a similar principle in mind when they announced in 1990 that they would create a minority scholarship fund of one hundred thousand dollars or endow an academic chair for minority students at each competing university; the aim was to induce colleges to participate in the Fiesta Bowl in Arizona, a state whose populace has refused to recognize the Martin Luther King, Jr., holiday.[25] Sunkist Growers, Inc., the event's sponsor, agreed to match the amount. Further 'sweetening the pot,' one university president promised to donate all net proceeds to university programs benefiting minority students."[26]

"Both examples," remarked Geneva, "illustrate how pocketbook issues are always near the top of the list of motives for racial behavior. That's why compliance with traditional civil rights laws is particularly tough during a period of great economic uncertainty, white nepotism becoming most prevalent when jobs and reasonably priced housing are

---

* A similar economically based principle underlay the action of the Connecticut Legislature when in 1973 it enacted a statute mandating penalties equal to the capital and operating costs saved by not installing and operating equipment to meet applicable regulatory limits.[22] In 1977, Congress added "noncompliance penalties" patterned after the Connecticut compliance program to section 120 of the Clean Air Act.[23] As of 1988, section 173(1)(A) of the Clean Air Act in effect permits the introduction of new pollution sources if "total allowable emissions" from existing and new sources are "sufficiently less than total emissions from existing sources allowed under the applicable implementation plan."[24]

in short supply. During such times, racial tolerance dissolves into hostility."

"Just as during the 1890s," I interjected, "when economic conditions for the working classes were at another low point, and there was intense labor and racial strife.[27] Today, whites have concluded, as they did a century ago, that the country has done enough for black people despite the flood of evidence to the contrary. The Supreme Court's civil rights decisions reflect the public's lack of interest. In the meantime, enforcement of civil rights laws, never vigorous, has dawdled into the doldrums, and this inertia encourages open violation and discourages victims from filing complaints they fear will only add futility and possible retaliation to their misery."

"All true," Geneva agreed.

"But given the already strong anti–civil rights trends," I argued, "wouldn't the Racial Preference Licensing Act simply encourage them?"

"You are resistant," Geneva replied. "Don't you see? For the very reasons you offer, urging stronger civil rights laws barring discrimination in this period is not simply foolhardy; it's the waste of a valuable opportunity."

"Well," I acknowledged, "I have no doubt that a great many white people would prefer the Racial Preference Licensing Act to traditional civil rights laws. The licensing feature provides legal protection for their racially discriminatory policies—particularly in employment and housing—which whites have practiced covertly, despite the presence on the books of civil rights laws and Court decisions declaring those practices unlawful."

"It is even more attractive," Geneva said, "in that thoughtful whites will view the new law as a means of giving moral legitimacy to their discriminatory preferences by adopting the theory[28] that whites have a right of non-association (with blacks), and that this right should be recognized in law."

"On those grounds," I put in, "the act could expect support from white civil libertarians who think racial discrimination abhorrent but are troubled by the need to coerce correct behavior. Whites will not be happy about the Equality Fund, though these provisions might attract the support of black separatists who would see the fund as a fair trade for the integration they always distrusted.[29] But, believe me, Geneva, no such benefits will assuage the absolute opposition of most civil rights professionals—black and white. They remain committed—to the point of obsession—with integration notions that, however widely held in the 1960s, are woefully beyond reach today."

"Don't start again!" Geneva threw up her hands. "I understand and sympathize with your civil rights friends' unwillingness to accept the legalized reincarnation of Jim Crow. They remember all too well how many of our people suffered and sacrificed to bury those obnoxious signs 'Colored' and 'White.' I think that even if I could prove that the Racial Preference Licensing Act would usher in the racial millennium, civil rights professionals would be unwilling to—as they might put it—'squander our high principles in return for a mess of segregation-tainted pottage.' Victory on such grounds is, they would conclude, no victory at all."

"You mock them, Geneva, but integration advocates would see themselves as standing by their principles."

"Principles, hell! What I do not understand—and this is what I really want to get clear—is what principle is so compelling as to justify continued allegiance to obsolete civil rights strategies that have done little to prevent—and may have contributed to—the contemporary statistics regarding black crime, broken families, devastated neighborhoods, alcohol and drug abuse, out-of-wedlock births, illiteracy, unemployment, and welfare dependency?"

She stopped to take a deep breath, then went on. "Racial segregation was surely hateful, but let me tell you, friend, that if I knew that its return would restore our black communities to what they were before desegregation, I would think such a trade entitled to serious thought. I would not dismiss it self-righteously, as you tell me many black leaders would do. Black people simply cannot afford the luxury of rigidity on racial issues. This story is not intended to urge actual adoption of a racial preference licensing law, but to provoke blacks and their white allies to look beyond traditional civil rights views. We must learn to examine every racial policy, including those that seem most hostile to blacks, and determine whether there is unintended potential African Americans can exploit.

"Think about it! Given the way things have gone historically, if all existing civil rights laws were invalidated, legislation like the Racial Preference Licensing Act might be all African Americans could expect. And it could prove no less—and perhaps more—effective than those laws that now provide us the promise of protection without either the will or the resources to honor that promise."

"Most civil rights advocates," I replied, "would, on hearing that argument, likely respond by linking arms and singing three choruses of 'We Shall Overcome.'"

"You're probably right, friend—but it is your job, is it not, to make them see that racist opposition has polluted the dream that phrase once inspired? However comforting, the dream distracts us from the harsh racial reality closing in around you and ours."

As I did not respond, Geneva continued. "You have to make people *see*. Just as parents used to tell children stories about the stork to avoid telling them about sex, so for similarly evasive reasons many black people hold to dreams about a truly integrated society that is brought into being by the enforcement of laws barring discriminatory conduct. History and—one would hope—common sense tells us that dream is never coming true."

"Dreams and ideals are not evil, Geneva."

"Of course, they aren't, but we need to be realistic about our present and future civil rights activities. The question is whether the activity reflects and is intended to challenge the actual barriers we face rather than those that seem a threat to the integration ideology."

"That's all very high-sounding, Geneva, and I agree that we need a more realistic perspective, but how can I bring others to recognize that need?"

"We might begin by considering the advantages of such a radical measure as the Racial Preference Licensing Act. First, by authorizing racial discrimination, such a law would, as I suggested earlier, remove the long-argued concern that civil rights laws deny anyone the right of non-association.* With the compulsive element removed, people who discriminate against blacks without getting the license authorized by law, may not retain the unspoken but real public sympathy they now enjoy. They may be viewed as what they are: law breakers who deserve punishment.

"Second, by requiring the discriminator both to publicize and to pay all blacks a price for that 'right,' the law may dilute both the financial and the psychological benefits of racism. Today even the worst racist denies being a racist. Most whites pay a tremendous price for their reflexive and often unconscious racism, but few are ready to post their racial preferences on a public license and even less ready to make direct payments for the privilege of practicing discrimination. Paradoxically, gaining the right to practice openly what people now enthusiastically practice covertly will take a lot of the joy out of discrimination and replace that joy with some costly pain.

"Third, black people will no longer have to divine—as we have regularly to do in this antidiscrimination era—whether an employer, a realtor, or a proprietor wants to exclude them.

---

* Herbert Wechsler, for example, has suggested the decision in *Brown* v. *Board of Education* might be criticized as requiring "integration [that] forces an association upon those for whom it is unpleasant or repugnant."[30]

The license will give them—and the world—ample notice. Those who seek to discriminate without a license will place their businesses at risk of serious, even ruinous, penalties."

"It seems crazy," I began.

"Racism is hardly based on logic. We need to fight racism the way a forest ranger fights fire with fire."

"Sounds to me," I said, "like trying to fight for civil rights the way Brer Rabbit got himself out of Brer Fox's clutches in the old Uncle Remus story."[31]

"Something like that." Geneva smiled, sensing that she was penetrating my skepticism. "In a bad situation he lacks the power to get out of, Brer Rabbit uses his wits. He doesn't waste any energy asking Brer Fox to set him free. He doesn't rely on his constitutional rights. Rather, he sets about pleading with Brer Fox that throwing him in the briar patch would be a fate worse than death. Convinced that the worst thing he could do to Brer Rabbit was the very thing Brer Rabbit didn't want him to do, Brer Fox threw Brer Rabbit right into the middle of the briar patch. And, of course, once in the brambles, Brer Rabbit easily slips through them and escapes."

"So," I pursued, "even if civil rights advocates strenuously resisted seeing any benefits in the Racial Preference Licensing Act, they may have their consciousness raised so as to seek out other sorts of briar patch?"

"Exactly. Civil rights advocates must first see the racial world as it is, determined by the need to maintain economic stability. And then, in the light of that reality, they must try to structure both initiatives and responses. We need, for example, to push for more money and more effective plans for curriculum in all-black schools rather than exhaust ourselves and our resources on ethereal integration in mainly white suburbs."

Drawing a deep breath, she asked, "Do you understand?" "Understanding is not my problem," I replied. "It's conviction that comes hard. And selling your position will require real conviction on my part. Even so, before committing it to my book, I'll try it out in my next law review article."

"I rather think law review editors and many of their readers will see my point more easily than you. They, unlike many of you who have worked for integration for decades, may not harbor fond hopes of America as having reached a racially integrated millennium. And they may be willing to look for potential gain even in the face of racial disaster. Perhaps if *they* accept your article, you will come to see the merits of my approach."

"Geneva!" I protested. "I don't need a law review editor to give legitimacy to your far-out notions about race."

She smiled. "Let's just say that the editor's approval will give my approach acceptability."

"In other words, you're saying I'll see its merits if white folks think it is a good idea. I don't think that's fair."

"Don't worry, friend. We black women are amazingly tolerant of our men's frailties in that area. Speaking of which," she added, "I assume you will be sending me that new story of yours that tests black women's tolerance in the ever-sensitive area of interracial romance."

I told her I would transmit it quite soon. Geneva rose to her full six feet. Still smiling, she bent and kissed me before heading toward the door. "Though you are impossible as ever, I have missed you."

The usually squeaky door to my study opened and closed, still not rousing my two large Weimaraner hounds which, usually alert to the slightest sound, had slept soundly through Geneva's visit.

Could I myself have been sleeping and imagined she'd been there? No, there on my monitor was every word of our conversation, miraculously transcribed.

CHAPTER 4

The Last Black Hero

THE BOMB'S EXPLOSION AT THE ANTIRACISM RALLY WAS intended to wreak havoc. It did. Six people died. Dozens were injured. All were members of the militant, community-based organization Quad A (the African American Activist Association). Gravely injured in the explosion was the group's founder and leader, Jason Warfield.

The bombing, far from precipitating the demise of Quad A—the goal of the white supremacists who carried out the attack—brought the organization thousands of new members, millions of dollars in contributions, and a national prestige that ensured their programs would be taken seriously by the media, by potential funding sources, and by the nation as a whole. From being just another black leader with a small though committed following, Jason Warfield became a national hope and, according to some blacks, "a true hero for his people."

He surely looked the part; and his resonant voice and soul-stirring rhetoric only emphasized his deep commitment to black people. More important, he lived his heroic role. He had risked his life in every imaginable protest from month-long fasts to thousand-mile marches. He had been arrested and jailed and was the frequent target of threats and harassment.

Jason was fiercely independent and took enormous pride in the fact that he said and did what he wanted to do, despite the opposition of whites who viewed as a distinct threat his militant rhetoric and his growing support from blacks in all sectors. Those blacks applauded as whites winced.

In a talk-show interview made just before the bombing and frequently replayed after it, Jason said, "My goal is to see racism eliminated from America. Period. I know, though, that racism is such an important component in American life that I may not succeed. But," he added, "I am not deterred or discouraged. I plan to fight racism as long as I live."

In the same interview, Jason spoke of his earlier life. "Initially, I wanted to be a singer, serious music. My hero was Paul Robeson. People even thought I sounded a little like him. Then I read a book about his life and decided that a singing career, even if I made it"—and he laughed—"was a trap in this schizophrenic society which welcomes and admires the talent of a black person like Robeson, but rejects him for his race. That's why," he said sadly, "so many talented black people who seem to have it made start acting like such damn fools. It's not that success has gone to their heads. It's that after years of struggle to achieve in athletics or entertainment—fields that seem open to blacks—they come to see that the acclaim they receive is not for them, but for their talent. In this society they, as persons, are still 'niggers.'"

After working his way through college, Jason explained, "I decided, as Paul Robeson did, to go to law school. I worked in civil rights law for a few years. It was exciting, but I became frustrated with the law's proclivity for preserving the status quo even at the cost of continuing inequities for black people. It was too much for me."

"I understand," the interviewer inquired, "that Dr. King was another of your heroes?"

"In everything I do, I refer to King's writings, speeches, and especially his actions. He was my reason for turning to the ministry—I even went back to divinity school. King's life enabled me to realize—unlike most of my civil rights lawyer friends—that activism more than legal precedent is the key to racial reform. You can't just talk about, meet about, and pray about racial discrimination. You have to confront it, challenge it, do battle, and then——"

"That is what *you* do," the interviewer interrupted, "but what if every black person in this country adopted Jason Warfield's militant stance? Would universal black militance end racism?"

Jason shook his head. "Universal black militance would end black people. Whites could not stand it. Even now, many whites treat a militant speech—not action, mind you, but a speech, a presentation of rhetoric in public—like a revolutionary conspiracy. When even a small group of blacks gather for some purpose more serious than a card party, whites get upset. Dr. King was deemed a militant black, as was Malcolm X, Medgar Evers, too many others. You get my point."

The interviewer looked as though he had, but could not come up with a response.

"Militant black leadership," Jason continued, "is like being on a bomb squad. It requires confidence in your skills and a courage able to survive the continuing awareness that you're messing with dynamite, but that someone has to do it. One mistake, and you're gone! Sometimes you're gone whether or not you make a mistake."

The interviewer nodded. "But what are you saying about Quad A, given the history of black groups? I think of Marcus Garvey's 'back to Africa' movement of the 1920s, and Dr. King's Southern Christian Leadership Conference, both of which floundered after their leaders were imprisoned or killed."

"Yes, Quad A ain't no one-man band," acknowledged Jason, lapsing from his customary formal speech. "It's dangerous for black organizations to rely on the usual 'minister as messianic leader,' and we've learned to be ready to replace a leader at a moment's notice. That's why even though Quad A started in my church, we've delegated leadership widely within a broad organizational structure, so if anything happens to me, one of my deputies is capable of taking over. We won't miss a beat."

Now miraculously recovered from his injuries and scheduled to return to his leadership post in New York in a few days, Jason was no longer in physical pain. But he was suffering intense emotional distress as he considered how Quad A and black people generally would respond to an unexpected manifestation of his vaunted independence.

As he sat in his hospital room staring out at the Arizona desert, he saw the source of his emotional turmoil drive into the parking lot. Through his window high up in the sanatorium complex, he had an unobstructed view of her sky-blue Z-240 sports car ("my one extravagance until you," she had told him) turning into the parking area, hesitate at a seemingly filled row, and then whip into what had to be the only open space in the huge lot. Jason smiled as he mentally chalked up another small victory for Sheila's sixth sense. "It serves her so well in everything," he mused—well, almost everything.

Today might prove different. "Might," he said aloud to the empty room. Sheila was entitled to and expected a more definite response than "might." He owed his life to her medical skill, supplemented with her almost constant care. The anguish he was feeling now was caused not by his injuries, but by the doctor who had been responsible for healing them. That anguish was compounded by the debt he owed the dedicated group of deputies who, despite dire predictions that Quad A would collapse without Jason's presence, had kept the movement together during his long convalescence. He knew they expected him to return to the racial wars unencumbered by a new love—particularly one not a member of their group. A majority of those deputies were black women. "Why not?" he had always responded when the question of their gender was raised. "They're all smart, hard-working, committed." "And," a news reporter once added, "fiercely loyal to you."

IT WAS TRUE. They were loyal and knew he loved and respected them as they did him. Their relationships had many dimensions, none sexual. Romance was an occasional temptation, but Jason's years in the church had taught him about the troubles that followed romance with women in a congregation. Quad A's structure, while not reliant on one leader, remained too fragile to place at risk because of an affair.

After Jason's injury, the deputies had selected Neva Brownlee as acting director. Neva, daughter of a prominent Washington, D.C., surgeon, had resigned a tenured professorship at the Howard Business School to join Quad A soon after Jason organized it. She had been his chief associate, and her managerial and fund-raising skills, together with Jason's leadership, had made Quad A an effective force. Despite the deputies' suspicions that Jason's feeling for Neva—and hers for him—might be personal, their relationship had not developed beyond mutual respect for each other's competence.

Even so, Jason's reliance on Neva had grown over time, and he admired and depended on her counsel as well as organizational skill. While attractive in a soft brown-skinned way, it was her wit and intelligence that enabled her to quietly dominate business meetings and charm social gatherings. She seemed well prepared in every situation.

His doctors had requested Neva not to contact him about Quad A business during what they feared would be a long and perilous recuperation. They did not want to dilute his chances for a full recovery in the quiet of the remote Arizona sanatorium. Neva responded to her appointment as acting director by redistributing and sharing authority even more widely than had been the case under Jason's leadership. As a result, the other deputies and their staffs redoubled their efforts.

Neva, having lunch with her mother, poked thoughtfully at her tuna salad as she explained that she had not heard from Jason in the more than ten months since he had left. "I don't think it's his fault—but, Mom, I must admit Jason's silence is strange. Even a few words of support and encouragement would be helpful. He must know this. It's not at all like him."

"Is that all?" her mother probed.

"Oh, Mom, not you, too! The Quad A deputies are treating me as though I've been jilted by Jason. We were working associates, friends, and that's it!"

"It's understandable. You two worked so closely together—and you do make a splendid-looking couple. No wonder some of your friends were skeptical when you told them you were joining Quad A just out of respect for the work Jason was doing."

"I guess it may have seemed that way, considering I was giving up a tenured position at a good school, selling my house, and moving myself from D.C. to New York. But, Mom, I was really excited about Quad A's potential for a new kind of civil rights organization. We look to ourselves for everything—skills, money, workers, lawyers, everything! My feelings for Jason are based on mutual respect and the strong bonds of friendship that developed over our years of shared struggle. I love my work, and I like and respect the man I work with." Neva paused, then added wryly, "Given my romantic history, that may be about the best I can hope for in a relationship."

Her mother nodded. Both recalled Neva's marriage soon after she finished college. Quite simply, it had been an unmitigated emotional disaster. A handsome, talented man, her husband had been immature and threatened by her intelligence. A second marriage had also ended when Neva discovered her husband engaged in an affair that had preceded her meeting him and not ended after the marriage.

"Two failed marriages in seven years told me clearly that my work—not romance or marriage—would prove the reliable foundation in my life. Oh, I brooded about it for a time, but finally came to agree with you when you said to me one day when I was really low, 'Listen, honey, it takes an extraordinary man to be better than no man at all.' And, Mom, I think of that each time a friend's seemingly enviable relationship breaks up because the man has acted like a bully, a dog, or a fool."

"That's good abstract advice," her mother cautioned. "It doesn't tell me how you feel about Jason's silence. Have you tried to reach him?"

"Several times. It's impossible to get through, and he doesn't answer my letters." Neva sighed. "Well, the medical reports indicate he should be released quite soon. I'll just have to wait—and so, Mom," she smiled, "let's stop the interrogation and talk about something else."

Under other circumstances, Neva Brownlee and Sheila Bainbridge might have been close friends. They certainly shared similar characteristics: intelligence, persistence, and commitment. Their backgrounds, though, were the exact reverse of what one might have expected. Neva, though black, was the child of professional parents who raised her in mainly white, upper-class neighborhoods. Until she entered Howard University, she had attended mainly white schools. Her interest in racial issues developed late, but finally gained priority over her business ambitions.

Sheila, on the other hand, white and born privileged, had been raised by her mother in a succession of small apartments in Queens and the Bronx. When she was two, Sheila's wealthy father had abandoned her mother who, fiercely proud, refused to seek her husband's financial help, determining to raise Sheila alone while working in secretarial jobs. Sheila learned both how her black and Hispanic peers felt and reacted to racial discrimination, and came to understand herself the meaning of minority status. She was not ashamed to be white, but her closest friends growing up were black or Hispanic. Majoring in black studies in college reflected both her academic interests and her already developed commitment to racial issues.

With a mother's tutoring, Sheila's quick mind and compulsive study habits enabled her to transcend the uneven education available in the public schools. Aided by a series of scholarships, she—like a growing number of young professional students—resolved her dual attraction to both law and medicine by earning degrees in both professions.

Medicine had proven the greater challenge, and her work with traumatic injuries at Harlem Hospital had won her both respect among her peers and a staff position at the Arizona hospital that specialized in the treatment of the seriously injured. It was there that Jason was brought and placed under her care.

JASON GLANCED AT his watch. Sheila had left town for two weeks and promised to return at four that afternoon. It was now just a few minutes after two. Did she plan to surprise him by arriving early? Not like her. She knew as well as he what was at stake. He watched her leave the car and then walk away from his building and toward a small park that overlooked the miles-long expanse of the artificial lake that provided welcome relief to the endless cactus and desert.

During the last few months when he had been able to walk again, Sheila had accompanied him to that small park on innumerable occasions. And there she had announced one evening, "You know, Jason, your recovery is going extremely well, but I'm turning over your medical care to another doctor."

At his look of hurt and surprise, she explained, "It's both unwise and unethical to have a love affair with your patient."

Jason protested, "We've talked, we've held hands, but there hasn't been any, you know——"

"There hasn't been any, and that's the point," Sheila said. "I don't know where our relationship is going, but I can't pretend that seeing you as frequently as I do is solely for your care and treatment. Freed of my medical responsibility, I hope we can be friends, discuss all the things we share and care about, and see where it leads."

After that evening, they walked a great deal and talked daily on that park bench. As their feeling for each other grew, they found they didn't have to talk all the time but were comfortable sitting in silence, looking out over the water toward the mountains far off in the distance. Even after acknowledging their love for one another, they recognized that the social barriers to their relationship were as serious as those facing Romeo and Juliet. "But," Jason assured Sheila and she agreed, "we—unlike Shakespeare's doomed lovers—are not teenagers. We are mature adults committed to our professional missions in life."

Now Sheila sat on their bench and contemplated alone the scene they had so often shared. Seeing her even from a distance reminded him of how much he had missed her. He was tempted to go down, join her in the park, and tell her so. He hesitated. She had carved out this time to think, to prepare herself to hear his response to her proposal, made before she left town, that she return to New York with him.

"Despite our love," she had said, "I think I know all the reasons you may never ask me to marry you. It is such a hateful paradox. You have fought racial barriers imposed by whites. Yet your concern about a barrier erected by blacks threatens our future together. I cannot and will not change what I am: a white woman. But, Jason, I reject all the privileges society has bestowed upon me because of my race, and accept willingly all the burdens of yours, including a decision that you must return to your work without me. This is presumptuous, but I want to go back with you. I think I can find work in New York, and I know I can make you happy."

Jason glanced at his watch. A quarter to four. He looked out the window. Sheila was still sitting in the park, but in a few moments she would leave and enter his building. He could almost hear her familiar knock at his door.

Jason closed his eyes and, as much in inquiry as in prayer, asked, "Lord, why was I spared? By every estimate, the bomb that exploded near the podium where I was standing should have killed me. Others died. I live. Why? Surely, I was not saved to fall in love with Sheila and make her, rather than my death, the instrument that will—as the bomb didn't— destroy Quad A?"

He sat in quiet contemplation. He had explored all the issues. Surely the answer he sought could be found both in Moses' tablets and in Jesus' clear and seemingly simple teachings. His Sermon on the Mount was his greatest miracle. Religious belief aside, it contained sufficient wisdom to sustain and uplift any life. But, in fact, those teachings condemned Jesus to the cross. The religion He inspired— founded in His Hebrew heritage—had led as many souls to destruction as salvation. And yet the slave singers in the Old South had been sufficiently touched by the message in Matthew 7:7 to fashion it into a hymn of faith: "Ask, and it shall be given you; seek and ye shall find; knock, and it shall be opened unto you." Jason smiled as he hummed the spiritual and waited for his answer to come.

LONG BEFORE RECEIVING the anonymous letter with the photograph of Jason and Sheila seated on the park bench, their arms entwined, Neva had sensed that his long silence reflected something more than hospital policy. The picture, though grainy and blurred by the telephoto lens used in its surreptitious shooting, clearly revealed two people very much in love. The writer of the typed note threatened to send copies of the print to the other Quad A deputies unless Neva purchased the negative at a large price which she knew would only guarantee future demands for more money.

Requesting that she not be disturbed, Neva closed her office door and for an hour allowed alternate waves of pain and rage to sweep through her. She was beyond tears. "How could you do this to me, to us, to them?" There was no answer, and she knew deep down that no answer would suffice. She recognized as well that there was time for neither grief nor rage. It would be better if Quad A's staff learned from her about the photograph and heard her deny its implications. She resolved to meet with them later today and remind them of the seriousness of Jason's injuries and that the note said the woman was his doctor. Jason hugged everybody. This embrace could have been gratitude rather than passion. She would urge them to wait until he returned to explain. She, too, would try to wait.

Late that night, Neva reviewed the long day's events with her mother.

"That was a courageous thing you did today, Neva. I'm proud of you."

"I don't deserve praise, Mom. I'm so angry, so hurt. I tried to explain that photo, but as impossible as it seems, I'm afraid that Jason, my boss, my hero—yes, someone who, if things had worked out, might have become my love—this man is going with a white woman.

"You know, Mom, we black women are always being reminded of how marginal and unworthy we are. We're never smart enough or beautiful enough or supportive, sexy, understanding, and resourceful enough to deserve a good black man."

"But, Neva," her mother protested, "suppose Jason's doctor had been black, would you feel less hurt?"

"You're damn right I would! Sure, I'd be disappointed that, after working four years with me, he chose someone else without even giving our relationship a chance, but I wouldn't feel rejected as a person."

"You shouldn't jump to conclusions about Jason that you urged Quad A's members to put aside until he returns," her mother counseled.

"Oh, he loves her all right! And he *will* bring her back here. I know Jason."

"And will you then resign?"

Neva shook her head. "I just don't know. I'm afraid Quad A would not survive my departure. I don't want to do that to the millions of black people who can benefit if Quad A continues its programs. Moreover, it would simply confirm what many in the group will think: that Jason has betrayed Quad A and me.

"In fact," she continued, "he may have discovered what I've been trying to get across to Quad A's deputies during the last year: that true love knows no boundaries of race and politics. For black women in particular to hold the view that we can never marry a white man is the real legacy of slavery and an unjustified restriction on choices already rendered far too narrow by the society's devastation of so many black men.

"If you can believe it, Mom, I've been urging more tolerance of black people who choose interracial love and marriage."

"And now Jason has given you the chance to prove you're ready to practice your egalitarian theory," her mother said. "It's a terrible choice, but one you needn't make tonight. Why not wait a few days before you decide?"

"Waiting isn't my style, Mom. And I've been working my tail off for over a year building this organization and readying it for a big push when Jason returns. Now he has put all of our efforts in jeopardy, and for what? No, Mom, I can't just wait, though Lord knows what I should do!"

"I have faith you'll do what's best, dear."

"Remember, Mom," Neva said wearily, "you warned me once that in a racist society, our black men's self-esteem is under constant attack, so that black women should be a source of strength and comfort for them."

"I continue to believe that's our responsibility."

"Perhaps," Neva said quietly. "But, Mom, how do we accept our responsibility in the face of betrayal and maintain the respect that was a basis for our love and caring in the first place?"

SHEILA SAT STARING at the lake without really seeing it. The two-week "vacation" she had told Jason she was taking to give him space to consider her marriage offer was only part of the reason for her West Coast trip. She had also been searching for a new job. Hospital officials, appalled at her so obviously having some sort of relationship with a patient, and a black one at that, had suspended her, allegedly for violating their doctor-patient regulations. She knew she had been scrupulous in her dealings with Jason while he was her patient, and understood that racism was the real reason for their censure. She told them as much in her letter of resignation, an action that—as she had discovered on her trip—would not make it easier to find another position.

At this moment, though, her thoughts were on Jason and the agony her proposal was causing him. "What," she asked herself, "does a man who is decisive and fearless do when he is rendered indecisive and afraid?" She knew he was deeply concerned about the fate of Quad A, of the black community, and of his place in history. But he was, after all, Jason Warfield, the last black hero, fearless and decisive. He would marry her and make it work for him, for them. Won't he? Shouldn't he? Is he not his own man?

For a brief moment, her spirits soared on the wings of optimism and then, pierced by an arrow of reality, spiraled down to earth with a pit-of-the-stomach-jarring thud. Why had she done it? Love was the easy answer, but she was old enough to understand the thrust of the title to Tina Turner's hit song "What's Love Got to Do with It?" What, indeed? Love is more than a passion that flows with an energy of its own and eschews any sense of responsibility. Real love connotes commitment and the acceptance of responsibility.

She had offered to marry him, she said, to give him a choice, but it was the cruelest of Hobson's choices—the kind of choice, she realized, white people give blacks all the time. "You can have this job, promotion, house, membership, provided you subordinate your thinking to ours and don't make waves on racial issues. Be acceptable and, if possible, grateful."

Her proposal was not as condescending as many; but had she been totally honest, her marriage proposal should have been, "Jason, I love you and want to marry you. In conformity with the age-old pattern of black sacrifice to serve white needs, will you risk your leadership role in Quad A and the respect you've earned in the black community in return for my love?"

Sheila shuddered and shook her head. "No!" she said aloud to the desert air. She simply would not use her love for him or his for her as the basis for perpetuating in their relationship the pattern of black sacrifice. She must give him his freedom whether he wanted it or not. Her decision made, Sheila rose wearily from the park bench and started toward the hospital. Then, eyes brimming with tears and her determination wavering, she returned to the bench and cried. Finally, she dabbed her eyes dry with her handkerchief. It was almost four o'clock. Jason was expecting her.

One of Jason's admonitions to Quad A members was to make sacrifices for the things you believe in. Well, she was giving up Jason for her belief in what? Not Quad A, whose members would never believe her love for him was real. Not even for Jason, whose terrible ambivalence had made her decision necessary. No, she was making this sacrifice for her belief that it was right. Painful, but right.

THE KNOCK ON his door relieved Jason's tension. Uncertain though he remained, he felt he would make the right decision.

"Come in, Sheila," he called.

The door opened, and a soft voice asked, "May I come in?"

"Neva, how did you get . . . ?" Jason's voice trailed off in the shock of seeing her. He realized suddenly how much he'd missed her.

"Hello, Jason," said Neva as calmly as she could in the equal shock of seeing him after so many months. "I decided it was time to take you home, and I flew out this morning." She bit her lip, fighting to control emotions that—kept in rein since she had received the letter—now threatened to overwhelm her.

"It's great to see you." Jason was standing now.

"I'm afraid, Jason, that what some of us consider bad news travels fast." She opened her bag and brought out the blackmail letter, the grainy photograph, and a copy of the statement she had made to top Quad A members. Her hand trembling, she handed him the envelope. "I think you should take a look at these, and then whatever you want to tell me I guess I'm ready to hear."

Jason felt weaker than he had in weeks. He read both letter and statement and then held them in his hand, wondering what to say.

Neva spoke first. "Lord knows, I have tried to understand—but, Jason, how could you allow yourself to fall in love with her? Did you think what it would mean to all the black women who idolize you, who pray daily for your recovery, who view you as their model of what black men should be?"

Neva continued, seeking to answer her question. "Oh, I realize that Quad A's work is frenetic, high-energy, intense, and crisis-oriented. Here, on the other hand, the atmosphere is relaxed and calm, and the relationship with your doctor is one of dependency and intense trust and intimacy. In this setting, you were far more vulnerable to a romantic relationship."

"Neva," Jason interrupted, "you don't have to make excuses for me."

"You misunderstand. I am saying that I can imagine how any seriously injured man might fall in love with his beautiful female doctor, but, Jason, you're not just any man. You are our ideal, our hero."

"It's a title I never wanted and should not have accepted. Lying in this bed, I realized that, in making me your hero, you wished to ascribe to me perfection I could never attain. By your attachment, you sought to gain a measure of that perfection for yourselves. I am Jason Warfield. I am not God in heroic form come to save you. The best I can do is to try and save myself and perhaps in my struggle serve as a model for you and others as you seek salvation in your own lives."

"But what kind of model are you Jason when you preach taking care of the sisters and then forsake us for a white woman? It's a departure from everything you said you stood for. I understand love is blind, but I don't see why you want to enter what will be a conflicted, uncomfortable relationship!

"Damn you for a hypocrite!" she said hotly. "Isn't it you who are always cautioning black men, 'Watch out lest the white woman come to represent a rite of passage to the status of whiteness? Because she's the model of beauty and femininity'"—Neva was mimicking Jason's deep voice, her arms folded, her legs apart in one of his characteristic stances—"'a white woman will appear to provide a black man with access to formerly restricted areas and also symbolize achievement. In particular, black men who acquire a measure of education, wealth, or status feel that dating white women is like moving out of the ghetto—a way of doing better for yourself.'"

"Just calm down, Neva," Jason said, on the verge of losing his famous cool. "I feel bad about disappointing you—and the others at Quad A. But I don't have to stand here and take your abuse. Hell, I've never advocated hate for whites as a component of our black pride program. Of course, we emphasize and encourage the forming and maintenance of strong black families as an essential for survival in a hostile racist society. But Quad A has never barred membership to interracial couples."

"No, Jason, but we do every damned thing we can to encourage black men"—she was mimicking him again—"'to look to the sisters,' as you said, 'and do not forsake them.' And, 'in black women,' you used to tell us, 'you will find both counsel and civility, love and support, friendship and faithfulness, probity and integrity. For the black man, the black woman is the equivalent of home.'

"There!" Neva concluded. "Just to show you what a fool I was, I memorized that homily of yours, believed it, preached it to others when—evidently—I should have been shouting it to you."

Despite herself, the tears were streaming down her face. Jason felt close to tears himself. He lowered his voice. "You didn't have to, Neva. I believed myself what I told others. I came here to get well, not to fall in love. I didn't want it to happen. To the extent that I considered entering a serious personal relationship with anyone, I guess it was with you."

It was, he realized immediately, a well-intended but ill-timed admission of his earlier interest in her.

"Now you tell me! Now you tell me!" Neva sputtered. "Is that supposed to be a compliment? Am I and other black women the Avis of sexual choice for you black men? 'Hey, black women, you are still Number Two! You will simply have to try harder!' Give me a break!"?

Unable to bear looking at Jason, Neva turned and stared out the window. Her breath was coming in sharp stabs, and in addition to her tears, her nose was running. She started to open her bag for a handkerchief, then stopped. To hell with it! she thought. The last thing I care about is looking good for that—that traitor. "Is it any wonder," she said more to the desert landscape than to him, "that so many black women view black men who choose white women with deep skepticism? Is it any goddamned wonder?"

"Neva, save the black woman rhetoric. I've heard it all before. But having a bomb go off almost under your feet, one that kills your friends and damn near kills you can change your outlook on a lot of things. Sheila literally put me back together. I was grateful, of course, but then I realized she's quite a woman, quite a human being. I feel really alive in her presence."

Neva turned from the window and stared at Jason, hearing him but not believing the strange words coming from that familiar voice. "You betrayed us! You told us over and over these five years that Quad A's work is too important to risk a relationship with me or one of the other black deputies. But now all your concerns evaporate, become mere 'image,' after a few months of close contact with a white woman. For her, you're willing to risk destruction of your organization as well as the hopes of vast numbers of black people."

Even through her anger, Neva realized that Jason had already answered her question. She tried to calm down and made her question more general. "Jason, tell me, why do the very men black women pray for—sensitive, successful warriors for truth and community, courage and integrity— always marry white women—women whose interest in our culture just happens always to include taking our most desirable men?"

Jason felt Neva's distress and wanted to help her. "I realize this is tough for you to hear. It was tough for me. I've imagined all manner of fantasies to explain how this could have happened."

"Such as?" Neva asked, skepticism clear in her voice.

"Well, you said yourself that recovering from my almost fatal injuries left me vulnerable in a way I was not back at Quad A. What if my injuries caused by the bomb blast had included blindness? What if, while I was recuperating in this remote place, Sheila had come as doctor and then become, as she has, the most important person in my life? My inability to see would not have insulated me from her warmth, her wisdom, her grace, and, after a time, her love."

Neva's sigh of dismay was close to a cry of pain. But Jason decided to continue. "Despite my oft-stated resolve to remain singlemindedly committed to Quad A, I might have fallen in love with Sheila's presence and then her person, without ever knowing until I regained my sight that she was not my ultimate African queen, as her melodiously throaty voice, her knowledge of black history, and her love of black culture would have led me to believe. If, in short, I had not realized Sheila was white, could I not plead some form of romantic entrapment?"

Neva sighed again and slowly shook her head. "Your deception defense won't work, Jason. In fact, it is more than a little insulting to me and to all black women. The sum of my existence is not confined to a knowledge of black history and a love of black culture. My identity cannot be so readily appropriated by *any* white woman—to the extent that even a blind black man would mistake her for me."

The silence that ensued after Neva's statement was interrupted by another knock on the door. This time Jason was sure he knew who it was. He sighed.

"Come in, Sheila."

For just an instant, Sheila was startled to see Jason had a visitor. Then she realized instinctively who the woman must be, why she was there.

Establishing her claim to Jason, she kissed him quickly on the forehead, then turned to Neva. "You must be Neva Brownlee. I've seen you on the news talking about Quad A. Welcome to Sanctus Sanatorium!" she said, trying for ease in what was clearly a thorny situation.

"So," Neva stated flatly, "you're Dr. Sheila Bainbridge."

Then, with one accord, the two women turned expectantly toward Jason. He, deep in his self-inflicted distress, hoped, for just an instant, that some undiscovered but devastating component of his injury might strike him down and remove him from this impossible predicament.

"Neva," Jason began slowly, looking at her, "I at least owe you candor. Sheila has been away for two weeks so we could each try to decide the future of what you have learned is our romance. Despite the sleazy source of your information, that romance is based on a love that is real. I am hoping we can be married soon."

As Jason looked intently at Neva, Sheila felt like an intruder eavesdropping on a conversation by her lover about their love—and thus hardly welcomed hearing either Jason's protestation of love or his decision to marry her. Deciding to follow his lead, she also addressed Neva.

"Ms. Brownlee, Jason is right. We are in love. But I have decided that I can't marry Jason—not because of his race, but because of mine. I know and think I understand how black people, and particularly black women, feel about losing one of their most able men in an interracial marriage. I'm afraid it would destroy Quad A. I simply will not do that to Jason or to black people."

Neva was furious. "Just a minute, Dr. Bainbridge! You need not play the martyr to save Quad A. We can survive and continue to grow whatever you and Jason do."

Sheila responded evenly, trying not to reveal her emotions. "My martyrdom, as you call it, may be as objectionable to you as your self-righteousness is to me. We both have strong attachments to the black community. And we both have suffered because of them."

"Given your knowledge of black history," Neva said, "you will understand that Jason is not the first black leader who has failed to live up to the people's expectations and hopes. I doubt he'll be the last. He has, in fact, provided us with a needed, if unwanted, reminder that human heroes have feet of clay."

Neva's words to Sheila hit Jason like a blow to the stomach, taking his breath, rendering him speechless. He remembered—too late—why he had determined not to get involved in any romantic situations at Quad A. And saw as well that he had himself fallen into the interracial trap he had warned other black men to stay clear of.

"When you reveal your relationship with Dr. Bainbridge," Neva continued, turning to him, "Quad A may have a rough time for a while. They'll know her only as 'that white woman.' But if you both return and she joins you in our work, there's just a chance that Quad A can equal the acceptance many black families achieve when one of their children marries a white person. I assume, Jason, that Dr. Bainbridge has qualities—other than her race—that attract you. In time, Quad A members may recognize them as well. Since, as I understand it, she is a lawyer as well as a doctor, surely she has skills we could use."

"You can't be serious!" Sheila interjected. "Quad A certainly wouldn't accept me as a staff member."

"On the contrary, Dr. Bainbridge, that may be the only way you can gain acceptance and perhaps prove that your concern for our cause is not limited to capturing one of our best black men."

"And what will you do, Neva, if we both return?" Jason asked.

Neva's control escaped her. "Isn't it a bit late in the game for you to become concerned about my welfare, Jason? After not hearing from you for a year, I assumed you didn't care how I felt as long as I kept your organization running for you. I'll do what is best for Quad A. Someone," she added, "has to give the organization priority over their personal feelings."

"You seem to forget, Ms. Brownlee," Sheila said with a hint of irritation, "I have decided not to return with Jason, and I'm certainly not going to disrupt Quad A by trying to join its staff."

"Oh, you'll return with him," said Neva. "Jason can be very persuasive when he wants to be. And I gather he wants *you!* I don't think there is anything either of us can do about that."

She stood and headed for the door. "I'm planning to take the late flight back to New York. I expect you'll let me know when you plan to arrive. I'll try to keep things going until——"

"Neva," Jason interrupted, "I owe you a great deal."

"Yes, Jason, you do, and I wish you didn't. I'll see you both in New York."

After Neva closed the door, Sheila and Jason looked at one another for a long time.

"Well," Jason said finally, "Neva was right. Quad A needs your medical and legal skills. I hope you will join our struggle."

She hesitated. "I would love to work with you and your group—if they'd have me—but I don't think I can compete with Neva one on one. It's obvious she came to see you as much out of devotion to Quad A as out of love for you."

"You don't have to compete with her," Jason assured Sheila. "We can get married right away."

"I've never believed the law of marriage could ensure a continuance of love."

"Then I'll resign from Quad A," he said with determination. "I do love you, Sheila."

"I know you mean that here, where we've spent so much time together, away from the real world. But you must return to your world, the only world you know. What will happen to our relationship then? It's awfully risky, Jason."

He took her in his arms and whispered, "Life *is* a risk, Sheila—and Quad A and you and Neva and I are all part of life. We might as well face up to whatever it brings."

Holding Jason close, Sheila took a deep breath and exhaled slowly. "Neva was right. You can be very convincing. But this has been quite an ordeal," she added, moving away, "and you should get some rest. I'll come back tomorrow."

She kissed Jason, again on the forehead, but with far less confidence than she had an hour earlier.

"And you'll make our plane reservations?" Jason asked.

Sheila hesitated at the door. Shaking her head in disbelief, she heard herself say, "Yes, Jason, I will make the reservations."

He sank down on the bed and for a long time simply lay there, staring at the ceiling, unseeing and numb. Both Sheila and Neva deserved better than the unheroic mess he had created by trying to do right in a situation where every choice was a snare, every decision a trap.

"Black hero, indeed!" he sighed to himself. "If that's how they viewed me, I certainly hope I am the last black hero. Our people must rely on their faith in God and themselves. Human beings may be able to *inspire* that faith. They cannot replace it and should not try."

He had prayed for life to continue the fight for his people's rights and well-being—a fight based on his confidence that he would intuitively know what direction to take, what policy to adopt, which to reject. Now his confidence was being undermined—or perhaps challenged—by, of all things, his involvement in an interracial romance.

Well, he thought, white folks will be pleased or, at least, relieved. Somehow, the once unthinkable act for a black man—marriage to a white woman—was now seen by whites as proof that black men in such relationships were, despite their militant rhetoric, not really dangerous. On the other hand, blacks—and particularly black women—felt generally as Neva did: betrayed.

He did not face this alone. Both Sheila and Neva would also have decisions to make, challenges to confront. Love was surely not the answer to America's racial problems, but who knows? Perhaps their decisions would suggest new policies that would reach both whites and blacks.

Jason pulled himself up, soaked a towel in cold water from the washbasin, and buried his face in its redeeming coolness. He felt better—not heroic, but better. He went to a closet and pulled out his suitcase.

As he began packing, the words of "I Don't Feel No Ways Tired" ran through his head—a favorite old gospel song, he remembered, of Neva's. Then, encouraged by its message and—strangely—by his memory of her humming it as she worked, he opened his mouth and sang:

> I don't feel no ways tired.
> I've come too far from where I started from.
> Nobody told me that the road would be easy.
> I don't believe He brought me this far, to leave me.

CHAPTER 5

Divining a
Racial Realism Theory

For as the body without the spirit is dead, so faith
without works is dead also.

—James 2:26

CRACK! ZING! THE SHOT AND THE BULLET'S RICOCHETING off the tree stump were almost instantaneous.

Then silence. I should have thrown myself down beside the log for protection. But I was too scared to move. I just sat, trying to recover from the shock. A year in New York City had made me wary of the numerous dangers that can befall its citizens there. But way out here in Oregon, surrounded by scenic beauty and the marvelous quiet of the deep woods? Well! I took a deep breath. Still shaking, I tried to get myself under control.

It was my first trip back to Oregon in several years. After seeing a few old friends, I managed to get away in a rented car to a national park in the Willamette Valley. I had left the car and walked for an hour along a seldom-traveled dirt road. The clearing I had selected was in the midst of a grove of old-growth trees. They stood like giant, two-centuries-old survivors of nature's challenges. But with the government's forestry policy now motivated by short-term greed, it was far from clear how long even the most beautiful of the old trees would be left standing.

Carrying only a light lunch and a briefcase containing my portable computer, I had hoped to do some writing in this scenic setting. Until a moment ago, it had seemed a splendid idea. Now, alone, an hour's hike from my car, I might be someone's idea of live (for the moment) target practice.

I glanced at the computer. The screen was still lit, but there was a deep, fresh gash in the log near where the computer was sitting, a dent I most certainly had not made.

"Sir, I'm very sorry." I looked up and there, not twenty feet away, was a sturdy white woman, probably in her mid-thirties. She was dressed in camouflage battle fatigues and sported a long-billed baseball cap over disheveled blonde hair. She exuded a sort of frenetic energy, which made the semiautomatic rifle in her hands seem all the more lethal.

"May I join you?" she asked, and again apologized, "I am truly sorry."

I managed to shrug my shoulders. Someone my age should, I thought, not allow himself to become this frightened. As she walked toward me, I took a few more deep breaths, hoping the air would clear my head, and finally managed, "Well, this gives me still another reason to favor strict gun control!"

"Liberals like you," she said sternly, "look to gun control laws to protect you from danger the way an ostrich looks for a hole to bury its head in. If prohibition didn't keep people from buying liquor, why do you think gun control laws will keep people from buying guns? All those laws will just bid up the price and increase the market for guns by turning a commodity into a possession even more prized because it's illegal."

When I simply stared at her, she added, "Well, don't you agree?"

"I certainly do not agree that guns should become a commodity, like TV sets or VCRs."

"Neither do I," she shot back, "but they will always be a popular possession in a society where gross disparities in opportunity, resources, and wealth breed frustration, violence, and crime."

I shrugged my shoulders and said nothing. That really set her off. "Shame!" she said vehemently. "You, a black man of all people, shouldn't be simply mouthing the traditional liberal line. I wasn't trying to shoot you, but there are plenty of whites who would like nothing better. What if I'd been out to kill you? I bet you're not carrying a gun, and that computer is proof that even an electronic pen is not more powerful than a sword—at least not out here in the wilds."

As my senses started to return, my annoyance surfaced. "Ms.——"

"Erika Wechsler, but call me Erika."

"O.K., Erika, your so-called wilds is a national park. And I came out here for peace and quiet, not to defend myself in a gun battle. I'm armed with the only thing I need to write and, while your shot just missed it, my computer is still functioning. So I accept your apologies, please be more careful with that thing, and good——"

"You can't dismiss a person with a gun, Professor," she interrupted, her voice level. "I'm not one of your students."

Startled, I asked her how she knew what I did.

"My father was a law professor. You talk like he did. And it's obvious you're as compulsive as he was, coming all the way out here to work when any sensible person would be simply enjoying the scenery. Plus, your folders read 'Constitutional Law class notes and Civil Rights seminar.' I mean, how many clues do I need?"

"Bravo!" I said wearily. "But, really, I need to get to work."

"O.K.," Erika said. "But, first, tell me what you're working on. Don't look so pained," she added. "I went to law school. Finished, too, for my father's sake. But hated every minute of it. Law practice wasn't much better, though my degree gives me protection against lawyers. They start all that technical crap on me, I look them dead in the eye: 'Buster,' I say, 'I went to law school, too. Don't give me that!' They usually straighten right up and talk sense."

"So," I hedged, "you're a lawyer, but don't like law?"

"Wrong. I'm fascinated by law, but law school teaches a great deal about appellate opinions and very little about the law."

I thought she'd hit the nail on the head, and said so.

"Hmm," Erika said approvingly. "Not many law teachers agree. Perhaps you're different. Still"—she gave me a hard look—"you're old enough to be one of those civil-rights–lawyer types who believe it's enough to rely on law to secure rights for your people. Am I right?"

"Yes," I replied, surprised, "that's what I was—once. For years I believed law was the answer, and I still teach law, including civil rights law. Now, though, I'm convinced that racism is a permanent part of the American landscape. The problem is that as soon as I express the view that racism cannot be vanquished by the enactment and vigorous enforcement of strong civil rights laws, most people conclude that I have given up, or surrendered, or, worse, sold out. Actually, I think they know better. The real problem is that my view—that racism is permanent—conflicts with and seems inimical to their world view. Moreover, many people, particularly civil rights advocates, have feared even to consider it—much less discuss it. Their reaction is usually reactionary and rarely grapples with the real question. I try to explain that a realistic appraisal of racism's crucial role in the society, far from being capitulation, would enable us to recognize the potential for effecting reform in even what appear to be setbacks." I thought of Geneva's Racial Preference Licensing Act, but decided not to go into its details with Erika. "At the least," I told her, "understanding the true nature of racism would equip us to weather its myriad harms."

"But, Professor, you're always dealing with theories and abstractions. Many of the civil rights veterans you upset are committed to the tangible, to what they see as real—including, paradoxically enough, traditional symbols like racial justice, equal opportunity, even integration."

"You're right, Erika," I acknowledged. "Having devoted much of their lives to instilling meaning, substance, even life into these concepts, they see their efforts eroding in the current reactionary climate. That's bad enough. Then I, a privileged law teacher, one to whom they look for encouragement, tell them—as they see it—that their beloved concepts were always empty, that they could never be realized. That's pretty scary stuff. All things considered, I guess I'm lucky they still let me talk—even though they refuse to listen."

Erika looked thoughtful. "It looks as though my stray shot was a happy accident rather than a near tragedy."

"Meaning?"

"Meaning that my work could prove of great help to yours. If I were you, I'd give me a few minutes to explain the racial realism project I'm working on."

"Two minutes." I looked at my watch.

"Good." She put down her heavy rifle. "Though it will probably take five minutes for me to tell you about my group. We call ourselves White Citizens for Black Survival, or WCBS. Our program has two prongs. First, the policy phase we call 'racial realism.' Then the activist phase, in which we aim to build a nationwide network of secret shelters to house and feed black people in the event of a black holocaust or some other all-out attack on America's historic scapegoats."

"A late-twentieth-century underground railroad!" I exclaimed. "You can't be serious?"

"You—and other blacks as well—need to *get* serious. What precisely would you do if they came for you? How would you protect your family? Where could you go? How would you get there? You have money. Could you get access to it if the government placed a hold on the assets in your checking and savings accounts?"

"I thought *I* was paranoid about whites, but you, Erika, a white, and a lawyer at that! Your paranoia is unnerving. How did you get involved with this group?"

"I'm one of the founders. We're a collective of whites dedicated to doing what we can to shield blacks from the worst dangers of racism. This may sound paternalistic, but it's not. To last in WCBS, one must try to be as sensitive to racial subordination as a member of the oppressor class can be: aware of what went on in the past beyond history's received truths, and cognizant of the fact that slavery, for example, tried to dehumanize blacks, and failed, and didn't try to dehumanize whites, but succeeded."

"The usual but almost never perceived outcomes of oppression," I interjected.

She nodded. "We understand it and are determined to avoid in ourselves the oppressors' penalty. We try to understand contemporary racism and the role it plays in American law, because law has always been a powerful expression of ruling interests. We believe that America's race problem is a white problem. We have determined to take personal responsibility for racism. Those of us living in isolated areas are in the process of altering our homes to hide, feed, and otherwise take care of black refugees. All of us undergo rigorous spiritual, moral, and military training. The last because we may have to launch attacks in order to defend blacks in a crisis."

"Shades of John Brown's body!" I said, in nervous jest.

But Erika, not getting it, asked, "How did you know that's what my brigade is called?"

I shook my head in exasperated skepticism. "This is too much! You want me to believe you've got white folks in military gear ready to take up arms against racism—which is to say, against other whites?"

"Like I said"—and she shrugged—"when you need us, we hope to be ready whether or not you believe in us. Our worry right now is not black people who don't think we're for real, but those people who know we are, including several far-right paramilitary groups and, of course, the U.S. government."

She paused at my look. "You don't have to believe me," she said. "But"—a purposeful edge crept into her next words— "we're among a very few groups—liberal, conservative, libertarian, what have you—to call the racial equality concept what it is—a hoax—and to mean it. To mean it so much that we refuse to participate in the society until there are major reforms.

"Like the Black Muslims or Malcolm X's ill-fated Organization of Afro-American Unity, which didn't live much longer than he did,* we believe we must articulate our

---

* Following his break with Elijah Muhammad, head of the Black Muslims, Malcolm X launched the Organization of Afro-American Unity (patterned after the Organization of African Unity). He said its basic aim was "to lift the whole freedom struggle from civil rights to the level of human rights and also to work with any other organization and any other leader toward that end."[1]

differences clearly even when our candor is upsetting to those who prefer diplomatic dialogue, based on tortured interpretations of history. Like the Black Muslims, we believe in separating ourselves from hostile environments. While we are not opposed to having blacks in our organization, we understand the danger of the presence of a few blacks possibly making us feel better about ourselves. And we don't want to endanger blacks any further than we already have by tacitly accepting and participating in a virulently racist society. We believe, moreover, that each race must take care of its problems before real multiracial togetherness is possible."

"So," I interjected, "if you have separated from blacks because you feel unready for interracial association, and from white society because of its hostile nature, how do WCBS members support themselves?"

"Easy, Professor, most of us have independent resources that enable us to work full-time for the organization."

"Look," I suggested, really interested in her program, "why don't I break out my sandwiches and fruit while you provide me with the details—or, at least, as many as you care to give—of the White Citizens for Black Survival's racial realism philosophy?"

But Erika hesitated. When I asked why, she laughed and said, "This outing of mine is supposed to include an all-day fast."

"O.K., given that WCBS is ready to die for me and mine, the least I can do is pass up lunch."

But Erika continued to stand.

"Now, what's wrong?"

"If you don't mind, Professor, I really should scout the perimeter. Just a precaution—it's in our manual, and . . . "

Her voice trailed off as my eyes rolled up in mock supplication. "Give me ten minutes. I'll be right back."

In her absence, I began to feel both foolish and nervous. This woman not only did not seem to be functioning on all cylinders but had a gun that posed a danger to anyone in her vicinity. I had packed my gear and was ready to head back toward my car when she returned.

"You're leaving?" And then, not waiting for my feeble excuses, she motioned in the direction I had come from. When I nodded, she said she didn't think I should start back right then. It was too much. I mustered all my dignity, and asked, "Is this another suggestion you expect me to heed because you're carrying a gun?"

"Of course not, Professor. It's just that—well, down that road a group of those far-right paramilitary types are having maneuvers. If they see a lone black man, they might decide you'd make a better target than those dummies they use. They usually leave about midafternoon, so you should wait here awhile."

I slumped back down on the log. "At this rate, I'll be happy to get back to the relative safety of New York City."

"Professor," Erika said, her calm voice not succeeding in masking her concern, "would you mind if we continued our conversation out of this clearing—perhaps in the stand of trees up on that little rise—so that, in case anyone comes this way, we'd have some advance notice?"

"No one back in Eugene told me these forests were danger-ous," I said, as I followed her up a slight hill and settled down between several large trees rather closely spaced together.

"They aren't—for whites. But there are very few black people in Oregon. Almost none down around Klamath Falls in southern Oregon, where this group is based. You would probably be O.K., but if I went along to escort you—given your antipathy to arms—and they saw us together, well . . . "

"Only in America," I suggested. Erika gave me a pained smile.

"Then," I asked, "you weren't just out here for a day of training. You were scouting the activities of this group."

"Well, I was doing both, but I think we're safe here. Let's forget the home-grown Nazis and talk about racial realism."

However outlandish she looked, Erika was clearly serious about her mission, and she did have guts. "More easily said than done," I told her, "but go ahead. We can talk and keep an eye out at the same time . . . just in case."

Erika began with a series of statements all too familiar to me: That the litigation and legislation based on the belief in eventual racial justice have always been dependent on the ability of believers both to remain faithful to the creed of ra-cial equality and to reject the contrary message of discrimi-nation. That, despite our best efforts to control or eliminate it, oppression on the basis of race returns time after time—in different guises, but it always returns. That all the formal or aspirational structure in the world can't mask the racial reality of the last three centuries.

"As you have probably noticed, Professor," she went on, "advocates of liberal civil rights theory tend to deny reality. The racial equality commitment has had to survive the undeniable fact that the Constitution's Framers initially opted to protect property, a category that included enslaved Africans. In addition, the political motivations for the Civil War amendments almost guaranteed that when political needs changed, enforcement of laws to protect the former slaves would likely lapse.* Even so, civil rights advocates continue to assume these amendments will eventually result in racial justice.

"These are the facts on which our racial realism theory is founded. Racial realism has four major themes, which tie in neatly with your thesis that racism is permanent. First, the historical point, that there has been no linear progress in civil rights. American racial history has demonstrated both steady subordination of blacks in one way or another and, if examined closely, a pattern of cyclical progress and cyclical regression.

"The second theme is economic. In our battles with racism, we need less discussion of ethics and more discussion of economics—much more. Ideals must not be allowed to obscure the blacks' real position in the socioeconomic realm,

---

* Interest in protecting blacks from continued assertions of white domination in the South had already waned by the time of the Hayes-Tilden compromise of 1877. Thus, the Republicans, to ensure the election of their candidate, Rutherford B. Hayes, in a disputed presidential election, were more than ready to agree to a compromise in which, among other things, they promised Democrats both to remove all remaining federal troops from the southern states and not to intervene further in "political affairs" in those states.[2]

which happens to be the real indicator of power in this country.

"Third, we believe in fulfillment—some might call it salvation—through struggle. We reject any philosophy that insists on measuring life's success on the achieving of specific goals—overlooking the process of living. More affirmatively and as a matter of faith, we believe that, despite the lack of linear progress, there is satisfaction in the struggle itself.

"Fourth, and finally, are the few imperatives implicit in racial realism. One is that those who presently battle oppression must at least consider looking at racism in this realistic way, however unfamiliar and defeatist it may sound; otherwise, black people are bound to repeat with their children what their grandparents suffered. For over three centuries, this country has promised democracy and delivered discrimination and delusions. Racial realism insists on both justice and truth. We are committed to truth and honesty with ourselves. We also insist on the possibility for justice, requiring that we shed reactionary attachments to myths that derive their destructive and legitimating power from our belief in them."

WCBS's views certainly did intersect with mine. "It's likely, though," I warned, "that merging those views will bring more hostility than enlightenment."

"New ideas always stir resistance. Look at your reaction to WCBS's mission to help black refugees in case of a general racial attack. You think I'm crazy. I see it in your eyes, and yet your view, that oppression on the basis of race is permanent, renders such an attack not only possible, but probable."

"Which is why so many people reject it. As a matter of fact, Erika, your racial realism is to race relations what legal realism is to jurisprudential thought."

"No disrespect intended, Professor, but I found jurisprudence boring in law school—too much theory that made the professor look profound, if undecipherable, and not enough real-world application of concepts presented with no context. Our philosophy is vibrant, based on experience, and motivated by our recognition of serious social wrongs. We do not purport to be academics. Law school is dry and disconnected with the reality of the real world, and it's overly reliant on appellate court opinions that once reflected real problems but now are preserved as legal precedent to be dissected and analyzed, like mummies in a tomb. They serve to justify preservation of the status quo while tending to bar social reform."

I told Erika she sounded a lot like the legal realists—that small group of legal scholars who, in the early 1930s, challenged the classical structure of law which was then thought of as a formal group of "common law" rules. Properly applied to any given situation, these rules were thought to lead to a correct—and therefore—a just result.* The realist movement was part of the general twentieth-century revolt against formalism and conceptualism, as reflected in the 1915 Supreme Court decision in *Coppage* v. *Kansas*,[5] which

---

* Legal realism has been seen as principally based in Oliver Wendell Holmes, Jr.'s, fifty-year battle against legal formalism.[3] The political Progressive movement, concerned with social welfare legislation and administrative regulation, helped push realism beyond Holmes.[4]

invalidated a state law that banned "yellow dog" contracts—
that is contracts where the workers agreed not to engage in
union activities. The Court reasoned that the Constitution's
due process clause gave workers a right to contract with their
employers. The realists saw it as the issue of whether indus-
trial workers in fact have bargaining power to choose the
terms of their employment.

The Court adhered to formalistic thinking even during
the Great Depression, when any realistic analysis of the state
of affairs would have included some recognition of the desperate need for state intervention. People were starving, and
for at least half of the population, the economy held little
hope of future employment. Even so, the Court rejected several pieces of New Deal corrective legislation—including
even some laws favored by many business leaders.[6] In other
words, as legal realists recognized, the Court insisted on
venerating grand rules that had little to do with the modern
context of poverty and misery. In opposing such heartless
decisions, the legal realists were outspoken and active. The
legal historian Professor G. Edward White writes of them:

> Legal scholars who came to call themselves Realists began
> with the perception that many early twentieth-century ju-
> dicial decisions were "wrong." They (the decisions) were
> wrong as matters of policy in that they promoted anti-
> quated concepts and values and ignored changed social
> conditions. They were wrong as exercises in logic in that
> they began with unexamined premises and reasoned syllo-
> gistically and artificially to conclusions. They were wrong

as efforts in governance in that they refused to include relevant information, such as data about the effects of legal rules on those subject to them, and insisted upon a conception of law as an autonomous entity isolated from nonlegal phenomena. Finally, they were wrong in that they perpetuated a status quo that had fostered rank inequalities of wealth, status, and condition, and was out of touch with the modern world.[7]

"So," I further explained, "the realist attack on short-sighted and stubborn judicial formalism is quite like the realistic assessment we're making of formal civil rights policy. My position is that the legal rules regarding racial discrimination have become not only *reified* (that is, ascribing material existence and power to what are really just ideas)—as the modern inheritor of realism, critical legal studies, would say—but *deified*. The worship of equality rules as having absolute power benefits whites by preserving a benevolent but fictional self-image, and such worship benefits blacks by preserving hope. But I think we've arrived at a place in history where the harms of such worship outweigh its benefits."

"Let me see if I understand," Erika interrupted. "In legal theory, the Supreme Court's notions about workers and employers each having a right to contract seemed to protect both from outside interference, though in economic fact the workers were at the mercy of exploitative employers. So today, while civil rights laws seem to protect blacks from bias, discrimination in fact continues under a myriad of guises, most of them either not covered or not easily ascertainable under existing laws. Affirmative action policies intended to compensate for the inadequacy of civil rights laws, are challenged by the claim that the mere presence of the civil rights statutes guarantees racial equality."

"Exactly," I agreed. "This is another way of saying that 'the law in action' does not reflect 'the law on the books.'[8] A parallel criticism that supports my thesis—that, in fact, helped me to conclude the intractability of racism—came from another law professor, the late Arthur S. Miller, who argued that there are really *two* Constitutions: one, the 'law on the books,' the actual, formal document, the highly acclaimed legacy of the Founding Fathers; the other, the 'law in action,' which consists of the informal understandings and conventions that actually determine social and governmental policy.[9] Unfortunately, save for an enlightened period during the 1950s and 1960s, most of the Supreme Court's decisions during the last twenty years seem based on the old formalist thinking."

"That's crazy!" Erika objected. "Why do they do that? How can they get away with it?"

To answer both questions, I cited the 1978 *Bakke* case,[10] where the Supreme Court invalidated the policy of California's medical school of reserving 10 percent of its openings for minorities. The Court relied heavily on the Fourteenth Amendment which the Court—during its enlightened period—said poses serious problems to state laws and policies that make racial classifications. In rigidly applying this rule in a seemingly neutral way to California's 10-percent minority admissions policy, a policy intended to make amends for years of overt discrimination, the Court's majority utterly ignored the fact that the white race had in fact the power and advantages; and that, notwithstanding the Fourteenth Amendment, the black race has for decades been denied entry into California's medical schools.

"The Court introduced," I went on, "an artificial and inappropriate parity in its reasoning—that is, that blacks and whites applying to medical school have always been treated equally in a state that has never practiced racial discrimination—and thus chose to ignore historical patterns, contemporary statistics, and flexible reasoning. It could then self-righteously deplore giving special privileges to any race in the admissions process."

"But what happened to realist thinking, Professor? The Court certainly didn't apply it in *Bakke,* and the *Bakke* decision was deemed fair and just by most white Americans. In fact, had it gone the other way, many people would have called for a law barring affirmative action."

"In a way," I answered, "the basic validity of the realist model is proven by its inability to gain acceptance in the legal marketplace—that actual power relations in the real world are by definition legitimate and must go unchallenged.[11] So, Erika, the realists would not have been surprised at the outcome in *Bakke.* They would recognize that, despite the realist challenge that destroyed the premises of the basic formalist model of law, that model survives, although in bankrupt form.[12]

"In addition, the realists suggested that the whole liberal world view of (private) rights and (public) sovereignty mediated by the rule of law needed to be exploded; such a world view, they argued, is only an attractive mirage masking the reality of economic and political power.[13] And the attack had profoundly threatening consequences; it carried with it the potential collapse of legal liberalism. In reaction, a spate of jurisprudential responses emerged defensively to combat what they perceived to be the realist attack on sacrosanct values and principles.[14]

"But, Erica, it wasn't that the realists wanted to destroy democratic values, as their critics charged. The realists were concerned with making the law more responsible to or reflective of society. They were committed to the investigation of facts and consequences instead of the old attachment to legal principles they deemed empty. And despite accounts that say realism failed because it advocated ethical relativism in a world where Nazi totalitarianism produced a longing for moral certainty, many realists were committed reformers. So, while they were labeled heretics, they were actually truth tellers."[15]

"Isn't there a parallel, Professor, between the formalists' reactionary faith in their supposedly apolitical principles and the modern captivation with colorblind neutrality? Pretty packaging does not make rules useful or effective and often ends up hiding what it purports to eliminate. At best, the law—by protecting blacks from blatant racist practices and policies, but rationalizing all manner of situations that relegate blacks to a subordinate status—regularizes racism."

"Of course!" I exclaimed, agreeing with her analysis. "And, as we have seen, even the laws or court decisions that abolish one form of discrimination may well allow for its appearance in another form, subtle though no less damaging. Thus, the *Brown* decision invalidated 'separate but equal,' replacing it—as civil rights advocates urged—with 'equal opportunity.' But given the continued motivations for racism, the society has managed to discriminate against blacks as effectively under the remedy as under the prior law—more effectively really, because discrimination today is covert, harder to prove, its ill effects easier to blame on its black victims."

"As we say," Erika put in, "it's a delusion to hope that things will get better if we can win this case or that one. That's why WCBS has called for a redefinition of the goals of racial equality and opportunity to which blacks have adhered for more than a century."

Of course, as I told Erika, I had already reached the same conclusion. "We must challenge the rigid ways of the past, recognizing—as Judge Benjamin Cardozo declared in 1932—that 'the agitations and the promptings of a changing civilization' demand more flexible legal forms and demand equally 'jurisprudence and philosophy adequate to justify the change.'"[16]

"Impressive, Professor," Erica nodded. "You have just articulated where our WCBS group started from. We reasoned that traditional civil rights law is also highly structured and founded on the belief that the Constitution was intended—at least after the Civil War amendments—to guarantee equal rights to blacks. In conformation with past practice, protection of black rights is now predictably episodic. For these

reasons, both the historic pattern and its contemporary rep-
lication require review and replacement of the now-defunct
ideology of racial equality.

"Also," she added, "you need a plan to counter if you can,
or escape if you cannot, a political deal that sacrifices black
lives rather than just black rights."

"I can't imagine——" I began.

"But, Professor," Erika broke in, "this country's Constitution is the result of a political deal that condemned your
ancestors to continued slavery—or had you forgotten?"

"I have not forgotten. But, Erika, we're in the 1990s, not
the 1790s. Rhetoric is one thing, melodrama another." I
started to repack my briefcase. "I'm afraid this part of our
discussion will require more time than I have if I'm to get
back to Eugene before dark."

"You all ain't goin' no place!"

Caught up in our discussion, we had failed to keep watch.
Turning at the voice, I saw a huge heavy-set white man,
dressed for the Second World War, complete with helmet.
He was brandishing a gun even larger and more ominous
than Erika's.

Trying to ignore the gun, I looked at Erika and asked, "I
assume this man is not a member of your team?"

Erika shook her head and addressed the intruder boldly.
"Guy Jenkins, your people are playing soldier down the
road. Why don't you go join them?"

The man stood his ground. "Thought I heard talkin'
goin' on. Decided to check it out. And what do I find? A nigger and his nigger-lovin' white woman, that's what I find.

Goin' to take you prisoners and march you down the road for the boys to see what they out here in the woods getting ready to fight against. Commander will decide on your punishment. Now get on up and move on out!"

I started up. Leaning over, Erika held my arm, but kept her eyes on him. "No, Guy, we're not going to be marched down that road by you or anybody else. I advise you to get on your way."

"You must be jokin'. I got my gun in my hand, Miss Lady Soldier. Yours is on the ground, and you better leave it there. Now move out, or else!"

"I think we——" I started up again.

"No, sir, we are not moving! Guy, it's your move! You have the gun. Shoot us, if you dare. You won't get a medal, but you will catch hell when you bring the feds down on your whole operation. This man may be a nigger to you, but he is a noted law professor to the rest of the country. Killing him is going to embarrass some big white folks and make others of them mad. Either way, they're going to come after you. I know them, Guy. They'll hunt you down like a dog, make an example of you to show that they're not really racist. Are you really that ready to be a hero to your buddies down the road? They'll all leave your ass high and dry—and you know it."

Guy looked a little less certain. For just a moment, he glanced back down the road—perhaps seeking guidance from his commander via mental telepathy.

In that moment, Erika was on him. I have no idea what karate move she made, but in the bat of an eye, Guy had lost his weapon and was groveling on the ground, moaning in pain.

Coolly Erika picked up his rifle, deftly removed the cartridge, and tossed the gun at his feet.

"Now before I really lose my temper, Guy," she said levelly, "take your weapon and get back to your group. Tell them you lost the ammo clip and then tell them anything you want, but I want them gone before we get there in the next thirty minutes."

Guy said nothing, just got to his feet, picked up his weapon, then turned and limped slowly down the path towards his group of far-right nationalists. I told Erika I surely admired her expertise, not only in getting rid of the fellow and us out of danger but in handing him an excuse for his empty weapon so that he wouldn't have to let his peers know he'd been outfoxed, and by a woman at that. "And then, to top it all, you played on his fear of being discovered so he'd get them *all* to leave!"

"Appealing to self-interest works on occasion," she said. Then, nodding cynically toward my computer and my briefcase, she said, "You know, all the electronic gadgetry and fancy jurisprudential ideas in the world won't stop them. Racism isn't about sophistication. Combating it isn't about finesse, except in the most vulgar sense of making a shameless appeal to the predictable self-interest of whites."

"Impressive," I acknowledged, "but also damned scary. I understand now, Erika, what you and your John Brown Brigade are about. There are limits to what we can do with philosophy. You and I know that if the need is great enough, the rewards large enough, the temptation strong enough, we blacks can be sacrificed at will. A present fear sometimes, a distant memory always."

Erika decided to follow Guy down the road to make sure he headed in the right direction. She and I shook hands, and with a final wave she disappeared through the trees. I sat back. It had been an exhausting afternoon. I closed my eyes and tried to relax against the tree, far from sure I had energy for the hour-long hike to my car, particularly if the way back was through enemy territory.

———

"FRIEND, WHY ARE you sleeping way out here in the woods?"

I knew that voice. I opened my eyes to see Geneva peering down at me. Her amused expression told me she knew exactly why I was where I was.

"Damn you, Geneva! You're responsible for this whole thing! Where is Erika? Or, rather, is there an Erika, or was she only you in one of your other guises? Am I not entitled to one afternoon off in a scenic location without your supernatural harassment?"

"All I want to say, friend, is that I read your 'Last Black Hero,' sensed your, ah, predicament, and wanted to see whether you—as opposed to your hero, Jason—could maintain a proper relationship with a white woman."

"I hope you got more than that out of my story!"

"I did," Geneva replied, "but I also hope you took Erika's message seriously. For all the reasons you have been describing, black people may need places of refuge and whites to provide escape from future betrayals.

"And for all the reasons that led you to conclude that racism is permanent, the ultimate betrayal, for which she and her White Citizens for Black Survival group are preparing, could happen."

"I can't say that it can't or it won't," I conceded, "but it's surely hard to imagine how it could happen. There's another 'but,' too." I paused.

"What's that?"

"Even if I knew for a certainty that whites planned another massive betrayal of blacks, most whites—and some blacks—would not believe me."

CHAPTER 6

The Rules of Racial Standing

"I AM A TRAVELER IN A STRANGE LAND, AND DURING MY journey I approach a tall mountain. Though it will take me out of my way, I am drawn irresistibly to climb it. There is a narrow path leading to the top, but the mountain is very steep. As I reach its summit, I am exhausted and disoriented and, at first, do not recognize a strange sound I hear. It seems like a voice. Then, unmistakably, it is a voice: not near, not far and, despite the other-worldly atmosphere, deep and resonant.

"It is a little scary, but I can't help noticing that the voice sounds suspiciously like the actor James Earl Jones doing one more TV commercial voiceover. It really riles me how even one of the country's finest actors cannot escape the exploitative practice of overlaying the actions of the whites portrayed on the screen with the warm, rich voices of blacks. Damn! I thought. If Langston Hughes were now writing his famous poem, whose first line is, 'You've taken my blues and gone,'[1] he'd have to include black voices as well as black music—both shamelessly employed by whites for the usual reason: profit.

"But James Earl Jones or not, while I can see no one in the vicinity, the voice is now unmistakable: 'WELCOME, FRIEND. WE HAVE BEEN WAITING FOR YOU. ALL IS IN READINESS.'

"Surprised, as well as amused, I look around for the source of the voice. There is no one. But nearby has materialized a glass-walled office, and on a desk in the very center of the room stands the most elaborate desktop computer I have ever seen. I enter the room and sit down at the computer. Immediately its screen flashes a command: 'SPEAK UP, IKE, AN 'SPRESS YO'SE'F!'

"I smile as I recognize the directive from one of Paul Lawrence Dunbar's dialect poems.[2] Though I've never felt autobiographical, my first hesitant words lead to a flood of sentences, paragraphs, pages about my life, my work. The longer I type, the faster come the pages. Time passes, but I feel neither weariness nor want. Finally, many hours later, I finish. I gather up the printed pages, which the computer produced silently and swiftly as I typed. As I walk from the room, I see before me a great light. I recognize the voice that greeted me on my arrival. It answers my questions before I have formed them:

YOU ARE HERE BECAUSE YOU ARE DEEMED WORTHY. WE HAVE READ THESE PAGES AND DISCERNED IN THEM YOUR TRUE MISSION. APPROACH THE LIGHT.

There is a loud but melodious sound like a crashing of celestial cymbals. The light disappears but, in some strange way, remains with me.

THE LIGHT YOU SAW, AND SEE NO MORE, IS NOW YOURS. YOU HAVE BEEN GRANTED TO KNOW THE RULES OF RACIAL STANDING. TAKE THE PAGES WITH YOU. THE ES-SENCE OF YOUR WORK IS NOW TRANSFORMED INTO A DE-SCRIPTION OF YOUR GIFT. USE IT WISELY. GUARD IT WELL. AND REMEMBER, NO GIFT COMES WITHOUT A PRICE.

There is silence. Computer room and voice are gone. I come down from the mountain and continue my trip. Arriving home, I turn to the pages. Sure enough, my lengthy text has been reduced to five rules engraved in gold on bound parchment pages.

As I finished, I reached into a desk drawer for a small sheaf of bound pages and handed them to Geneva. "I dreamed the story I just told you and the next morning found these pages. I assume both the dream and the rules are your gift."

Geneva didn't confirm my assumptions, but the devilish look in her eye gave her away. "Why don't you read and con-sider the first of the rules. Then let me know your thoughts."

FIRST RULE

The law grants litigants standing to come into court based on their having sufficient personal interest and involvement in the issue to justify judicial cognizance.[3] *Black people (while they may be able to get into court) are denied such*

*standing legitimacy in the world generally when they discuss
their negative experiences with racism or even when they attempt to give a positive evaluation of another black person
or of his or her work.*[4] *No matter their experience or expertise, blacks' statements involving race are deemed "special
pleading" and thus not entitled to serious consideration.*

"Isn't this the point of *Invisible Man*," I asked, "where
Ralph Ellison depicts blacks as a category of human beings
whose suffering is so thoroughly ignored that they, and it,
might as well not exist?"[5]

"Quite right. Ellison's novel was published forty years
ago," Geneva replied, "and despite all the acclaim it received,
the number of black people suffering because of racism—
and virtually ignored in their suffering—has increased."

"In particular," I said, "the First Rule accurately reflects
the special discounting of black views when we recommend
other blacks for a position or for promotion. When not ignored entirely, the unconvinced response from whites will
contain the scarcely concealed question 'Who else likes this
person?' Both parties know *who* 'who else' is.

"Misunderstanding, though, poses the real danger—a
lesson I learned without the gift of a special rule. When
back in 1957, as my first lawyering job I went to work at
the Justice Department, only a few of the thousands of lawyers there were black. One of them, Maceo Hubbard, a man
of broad experience, taught me a lot I had not learned in
law school. 'When white folks ask you for an evaluation of
another black,' he warned me, 'you have to remember one
thing. However carefully you say it, you can hurt the brother,

but you can't help him.' Maceo's sage advice, unhappily, is still valid."

"I understand," Geneva said, "that, as a matter of course, some minority law teachers simply do not read and evaluate the work of other minority teachers."

"I don't go that far. For one thing, my failure to comment when asked is taken as a negative recommendation. But when law schools request—as they frequently do— that I evaluate the scholarly work of another black law teacher being considered for promotion or tenure, I approach the task with great caution. I remember all too well an instance when, younger and less wise, I wrote a generally favorable letter for a black teacher. I noted—I thought in the interest of objectivity—that because the piece under review had been prepared for a conference presentation, the paucity of its footnoting was acceptable. I was certain, I said, that the author would provide more support for his statements when the speech was revised for publication. The upshot was that not only was the professor denied tenure, but in explaining his supposed deficiencies to others—and to him—the faculty reported that they had no choice: 'Even another black law teacher said this man is not scholarly.' It was a painful application of Maceo Hubbard's warning. The candidate didn't speak to me for some years afterward."

Geneva shook her head sadly. "Great profession you're in."

"It goes with the territory of being black, not of being a law teacher," I said, turning to the Second Rule.

SECOND RULE

Not only are blacks' complaints discounted, but black victims of racism are less effective witnesses than are whites, who are members of the oppressor class. This phenomenon reflects a widespread assumption that blacks, unlike whites, cannot be objective on racial issues and will favor their own no matter what. This deep-seated belief fuels a continuing effort—despite all manner of Supreme Court decisions intended to curb the practice—to keep black people off juries in cases involving race.[6] Black judges hearing racial cases are eyed suspiciously and sometimes asked to recuse themselves in favor of a white judge—without those making the request even being aware of the paradox in their motions.[7]

I pointed out to Geneva that this rule is applicable far beyond black jurors and judges. It is no accident that white writers have dominated the recording of race relations in this country: they are considered the more objective commentators on racial issues. For example, the litigation leading up to the Court's decision in *Brown v. Board of Education*[8] has been well documented by Richard Kluger's *Simple Justice*[9]—as has the life and work of Dr. Martin Luther King, Jr., by David Garrow[10] and Taylor Branch,[11] among other white writers,[12] whose work covers the protest aspects of the civil rights movement. Black writers who have covered similar ground, however, have not received the attention or the rewards of their white colleagues.[13] The writer Gloria Joseph summarizes the problem as, having commended as exemplary a white writer's essay on feminism and racism, she then acknowledges that the white writer "reiterates much that has been voiced by black female writers, but the acclaim given her article shows again that it takes whiteness to give even Blackness validity."[14] The black writer and poet bell hooks articulates the frustration resulting from this phenomenon when she complains: "We produce cultural criticism in the context of white supremacy. At times, even the most progressive and well-meaning white folks, who are friends and allies, may not understand why a black writer has to say something a certain way, or why we may not want to explain what has been said as though the first people we must always be addressing are privileged white readers." Later on the same page, though, she acknowledges a deeper dimension to her frustration: "And [yet] every black writer knows that the people you may most want to hear your words may never read them, that many of them have never learned to read."[15]

"I think bell hooks speaks for all of us," I said, "and the worst aspect of our frustration is that the pressure to perform primarily for those for whom we care less is less part of some invidious scheme than an economic necessity so long repeated it is now a cultural component of life as blacks in a nation that is—despite all—determined to be and remain white."

"The black writer," Geneva suggested, "is not unlike the black mother who, to sustain herself and her children, must work all day taking care of white children while her own are neglected."

"These rules seem more like revelations of distilled woe than gifts. Let's see what comes next."

THIRD RULE

Few blacks avoid diminishment of racial standing, most of their statements about racial conditions being diluted and their recommendations of other blacks taken with a grain of salt. The usual exception to this rule is the black person who publicly disparages or criticizes other blacks who are speaking or acting in ways that upset whites. Instantly, such statements are granted "enhanced standing" even when the speaker has no special expertise or experience in the subject he or she is criticizing.

"Right on the mark again, Geneva!" I said, thinking of President George H. W. Bush's nomination of Clarence Thomas to the Supreme Court in the summer of 1991 as—the President claimed—the most qualified person for the position. Given Thomas's modest academic background, relative youth, lack of litigation experience, and undistinguished service in appointive government positions, only his 'enhanced standing,' in accordance with the Third Rule, as a well-known critic of affirmative action and civil rights policies and leaders in general could have won him priority over the multitude of lawyers, white and black, with more traditional qualifications for a seat on our highest Court.

Indeed, the Thomas appointment is a definitive, but far from the sole, example of the awards awaiting blacks who gain enhanced standing. Black scholars have watched in angry frustration while blacks like Thomas Sowell, Walter Williams, Glenn Loury, and Shelby Steele gain national celebrity as experts on race owing to their willingness to minimize the effect of racism on the lowly status of blacks.

"The fact that, in line with the First Rule, most blacks dispute these assessments is generally ignored," I explained to Geneva. "Of course, some white people will scoff at your rules of racial standing, dismissing them as merely an exemplar of the old adage 'Dog bites man: no news. Man bites dog: news.' And where criticism or whistle blowing by an insider wins immediate attention, any laudatory statement by a person affiliated with a product or an institution is viewed, to some extent, as special pleading."

"Shouldn't," Geneva asked, "all but the most insensitive be able to distinguish a peoples' plaintive efforts to protest racism from a company's product-enhancing puffery?"

"Perhaps—but, distinguishable or not, it galls me that black scholars who labor in relative obscurity can leap to instant attention and acclaim by criticizing their black colleagues. This happened when Professor Randall Kennedy at Harvard Law School asserted that minority scholars have no special legitimacy in writing about race, and that their scholarship, measured by traditional standards, is flawed.[16] Had Kennedy been lauding black legal scholars, his article would have been treated as just another piece of special pleading."

"But wait!" Geneva interrupted. "The several pieces I have read by Professor Kennedy are well done and tend to give white folks hell."[17]

"Precisely my point. None of those articles have been covered by the *New York Times*.[18] But don't get me started,

Geneva. Examples abound. In the fall of 1991, Professor Stephen Carter published *Reflections of an Affirmative Action Baby*,[19] in which he—who in 1985 had become the first black person to gain tenure at the prestigious Yale Law School—expressed serious reservations about the value of affirmative action for himself and others. Immediately, the book soared to national attention, and Carter began to frequent the television talk shows."

Geneva sniffed significantly. "Do I discern the distinct aroma of sour grapes?"

I threw up my hands. "Could be, but let me just say in my defense that the phenomenon of enhanced racial standing set out in the Third Rule is, while not called by that name, certainly well known. I think it's cause for wonder and more than a little credit to our integrity that more black scholars don't maim one another in a wild scramble to gain for ourselves the acclaim, adulation, and accompanying profit almost guaranteed to those of us willing to condemn our own."

"Are you suggesting," Geneva asked in feigned dudgeon, "that after all my effort your book will not leap to the top of the best-seller charts?"

"No outrageous attacks on blacks, no explicit sex, and no revelations of how bad black men treat black women! No, Geneva, I'm afraid you'll have to be content with your small, but very devoted audience."

Now she was genuinely indignant. "Wait just a minute, sir. Do you equate black women writers who describe the ill treatment black women have received at the hands of black

men, with the black scholar-opportunists who reap fame
and fortune by denying that racism is the cause of blacks'
distress?"

"I do not. Nor do I suggest that black scholars who gain
enhanced standing because of the anti-black or anti–civil
rights tone of their writing have taken their positions for personal gain. Some, perhaps all, actually believe what they're
saying. What I criticize is their refusal to come to grips with
the effect of their statements.

"As to black women writers who set out in fiction or fac-
tual terms the distressing treatment some of them have suffered at the hands of black men, the truth of their writing
is self-evident. But I wish they'd make clearer the point that
much of this ill treatment is the result of black male frustration with having constantly to cope with the barriers of racism, including systemic job discrimination that is the direct
cause of the brutal circumstances in which so many blacks
live their lives."

"Are they," Geneva asked, with only slightly disguised
scorn, "obligated to insert caveats reminding readers that
abusive behavior by black men is often motivated by frustration with the constraints racism imposes on their lives?"

"Of course not. But they should know that since at least
the 1975 publication of Ntozake Shange's *For colored girls
who have considered suicide when the rainbow is enuf*,[20]
there has been a market for writing by black women on this
subject—and, as you know, some of that writing has been the
cause of debate and accusations.[21] I think, though, that the
criticism and the potential for harm of black women writing

adversely about black men is not as damaging to the black community as the black scholars' writing against blacks. Actually, there's a more dire form of black self-criticism which may be covered in the next rule."

FOURTH RULE

When a black person or group makes a statement or takes an action that the white community or vocal components thereof deem "outrageous," the latter will actively recruit blacks willing to refute the statement or condemn the action. Blacks who respond to the call for condemnation will receive superstanding status. Those blacks who refuse to be recruited will be interpreted as endorsing the statements and action and may suffer political or economic reprisals.

"Pretty strong stuff!" I exclaimed.

"Meaning?" Geneva asked.

"Well, perhaps the best contemporary example of the Fourth Rule involves the adverse reaction of many whites to the Muslim minister Louis Farrakhan. Smart and superarticulate, Minister Farrakhan is perhaps the best living example of a black man ready, willing, and able to 'tell it like it is' regarding who is responsible for racism in this country. In this regard, he's easily a match for all those condescending white talk-show hosts who consider themselves very intelligent, certainly smarter than *any* black man.

"All these TV pros seems anxious to put this outspoken black man in his place. They have big staffs to do their research and prepare scripts filled to the brim with denigrating questions. And they have film clips carefully edited to make Farrakhan look as outrageous and irresponsible as possible.

"On camera, these self-appointed defenders of a society senseless enough to put them in their highly paid jobs, attack Farrakhan with a vengeance. Clearly, destruction and not discussion is their aim. But there's no contest. Minister Farrakhan, calm, cool, and very much on top of the questions, handles these self-appointed guardians with ease. I love it!"

"I gather," Geneva broke in, "that many black people do not concur in your assessment of the Farrakhan phenomenon."

"It doesn't matter. Whatever their views on the controversial Black Muslim minister, every black person important enough to be interviewed is asked to condemn Minister Farrakhan—or any other truly outspoken black leader. Reporters generally ask, 'Have you heard what Farrakhan said and what are *you* going to do about it?' Note that, with Farrakhan, it's not what do you have to say, but what are you going to *do* about what he said? And don't make the mistake of telling a reporter ten positive things about Farrakhan and adding one criticism. You guessed it, the story will be headlined: 'LEADING BLACK SPOKESPERSON CONDEMNS FARRAKHAN.'"

"But," Geneva objected, "Farrakhan is a Black Muslim, which most blacks are definitely not."

"It's not his faith we're asked to deal with, Geneva. It's his race and his mouth."

She laughed. "On the surface, this is strange, kind of crazy. Remember the biblical story of how little David killed the mighty Goliath. David left his sheep in the field, journeyed to

the impending battle, and convinced King Saul of the Israelites to allow him to be their champion. The armor they put
on him was so heavy, he took it off, and went to meet Goliath with his staff, a slingshot, and five smooth stones in his
pouch. And David was not modest or shy as he told Goliath
what the Philistine giant least wanted to hear:

> This day will the LORD deliver thee into mine hand; and
> I will smite thee, and take thine head from thee; and I will
> give the carcases of the host of the Philistines this day unto
> the fowls of the air, and to the wild beasts of the earth; that
> all the earth may know that there is a God in Israel.[22]

"For many people," Geneva continued, "Minister Farrakhan is a black David going one on one against the Philistines who bestride the land, abusing their power and
generally messing over black folk. But when Farrakhan issues his challenge, no Goliath comes forth. Rather, some of
the Philistines come running, not up to Farrakhan, but to
any black person of substance they can find, asking, 'Did
you hear what that man said about us? What are *you* going
to do about it?'"

"That's the question I've been asking myself, Geneva," I
responded. "Why must I do something about Minister Farrakhan? Those he condemns are not without power, not without money, not without guns. A sad history serves as proof
that they know how to use all three against us. Why me?

"'Oh,' I am told, 'that man is hurting your cause.' But
the cause of black people has been under attack for three

hundred years, not by one black man but by the dominant white society. The suggestion that our current plight would be relieved if Farrakhan would just shut up is both naïve and insults our intelligence. It also reveals more about those who would silence him than they likely want uncovered."

I went on with how, in 1985, when Farrakhan was scheduled to speak in New York City's Madison Square Garden, black officials came under heavy pressure to speak out and denounce him because of earlier statements of his deemed anti-Semitic and anti-white.[23] Some black officials spoke out. Others, while not condoning some of Farrakhan's comments, complained in interviews that they were repeatedly expected to condemn fellow blacks for offensive remarks or behavior, while whites are not called upon to react to every such indiscretion by white officials. Typical of this position, Representative Charles B. Rangel (D., N.Y.) told a reporter that Farrakhan's statements about Judaism being a "dirty religion" were "garbage," but added, "it's easy to come down heavy on Farrakhan." Rangel expressed the hope that matters had not reached the point that, just as blacks in South Africa have to carry a passbook to go from place to place, "black Americans have to carry their last statement refuting Farrakhan. I would not, if someone said Jesus Christ is a phony, go around asking Jews to sign a statement to condemn him."[24]

In a similar vein, the Reverend Calvin O. Butts, pastor of the Abyssinian Baptist Church in Harlem, refused to condemn Farrakhan, and pointed out that the Muslim minister criticizes many groups in strong terms, including black churches and black ministers. Butts acknowledged that many Jewish people "look askance at any slight breeze of anti-Semitism. However," he added, "if in response to Israel's refusal to impose sanctions on South Africa to protest its policies of racial separation, I jumped up and said all Jewish leaders in the United States should denounce Israel, how many Jewish people would join me in that? I don't think many."[25]

"I agree, Geneva," I said, "with both Congressman Rangel and the Reverend Butts. Anti-Semitism is a horrible thing, but just as all criticism of blacks is not racism, so not every negative comment about Jews—even if it is wrong—is anti-Semitism. Were I a Jew, I would be damned concerned about the latent—and often active—anti-Semitism in this country. But to leap with a vengeance on inflammatory comments by blacks is a misguided effort to vent justified fears on black targets of opportunity who are the society's least powerful influences and—I might add—the most likely to be made the scapegoats for deeply rooted anti-Semitism that they didn't create and that will not be cured by their destruction."

"Fear is not rational," Geneva observed. "Jews understandably feel that they must attack anti-Semitism whenever it appears. Farrakhan, being a frightening figure for most whites and thus vulnerable, becomes a symbol—even though, as you point out, an inappropriate one of the nation's anti-Semitism. Jews and white people generally hope that criticism by blacks will diminish his credibility, if not in the eyes of his followers, at least in the minds of those who believe that the threat he represents can be defused by our responding to their urgent pleas for black condemnation of an out-of-control black."

"It's not set out in the Fourth Rule, Geneva, but have you noticed that those blacks who utter 'beyond the pale' remarks are never forgiven. Thus, when Farrakhan attempts to explain that his statement was aimed at Israel as a state and not at Judaism as a religion, his explanation is rejected out of hand. The attitude seems to be: 'You said it, and thus you must be condemned for all time.'"

Geneva agreed. "The Reverend Jesse Jackson has experienced a similar 'lifetime renunciation' notwithstanding his frequent and fervent apologies for the regrettable 'Hymie and Hymietown' remarks he made during his 1984 presidential campaign.[26] As I indicated earlier, I understand why a group is upset by what it deems racial or religious insults, but I doubt that I'm alone in not understanding why blacks who lack any real power in the society are not forgiven while whites, including those at the highest levels of power, are pardoned. For example, many Jewish spokespeople complained bitterly when President Reagan went to lay a wreath at the Nazi cemetery at Bitburg in Germany,[27] but they do not continue to harass him about the issue everywhere he goes. No one denounced Reagan as anti-Semitic for going. More significantly, neither President Bush nor the whites who support him are called on to condemn Reagan in order to prove that they are not anti-Semitic.

"We boast that, unlike communist countries, there is no censorship of the press here. But blacks like Jesse Jackson,

who are subject to an unofficial but no less effective 'renunciation,' are simply not heard."

"Your renunciation isn't limited to controversial political figures," I interrupted. "The writer bell hooks complains that 'often radical writers doing transgressive work
are told not that it's too political or too "left," but simply
that it will not sell or readers just will not be interested in
that perspective.'"[28]

"Similarly," she continued, "one need not agree with Farrakhan that African Americans need to separate from this
country to understand that, after three hundred years of trying and not yet having the acceptance here that non-English-
speaking white immigrants have on their first day on this
soil, we need to be thinking of (if not yet doing) something
other than singing one more chorus of 'We Shall Overcome.'
Whatever his rhetorical transgressions, Minister Farrakhan
and his church are giving the most disadvantaged black folk
reason to hope when most of the country and more than a
few of us blacks have written them off. His television hosts
give him credit for cleaning up a neighborhood in Washington, D.C.,* and yet question his motives for accomplishing
what few government officials have even seriously tried."

Thinking of Geneva's earlier statement about blacks who
do not agree with our position on Farrakhan, I recalled a
black friend who was unmoved when I discussed Farrakhan's

---

* In 1991, the Nation of Islam and its Abundant Life Clinic received a cita-
tion from the City of Washington, D.C., for expunging Washington's Mayfair
Mansions of violent crack dealing. The Nation of Islam continues to patrol
the area.[29]

abilities, and said, "Even if everything you say about him is correct, he is still a bigot. Why can't I call him what I think he is?" In effect, my friend was asking, "Even given the perverse weight white society gives to black-on-black criticism, must persons of color remain silent if they strongly disagree with statements or actions by other blacks?"

"The whole racial standing phenomenon, Geneva, raises a troublesome dilemma for many black scholars. How can blacks criticize other blacks or civil rights policies with which they disagree? Must they sacrifice their academic freedom, even their First Amendment right to free speech, in order to prevent whites from endowing with super standing their assertion of anti-black beliefs they have held all along?"

"The answer," Geneva said, "is that a burden of blackness, particularly for the black scholar, is racial awareness. Black academics must weigh the value of their statements, their writings, against the fact that, like it or not, their criticism of other blacks—whether or not accurate, or fair, or relevant—will gain them enhanced or super standing. In some instances, they may feel so strongly about an issue or an individual that there is no alternative to speaking out—despite the predictable consequences."

"I don't disagree," I responded, "but those who decide that, despite all, they must speak out against blacks who are threatening to whites, must not be surprised when blacks subjected to public criticism, cry 'Foul.' And when the black critics are later criticized themselves, this is not intended to—and certainly does not—silence the black speakers, as is claimed by Professor Stephen Carter.[30] After all, they now have enhanced or super standing. White people want to hear their views, almost ad nauseam. Rather, some of the rest of us are saying, 'Now, see what you have done. Knowing the consequences, you should have communicated your criticism in some other way.'"

"Is there an inconsistency," Geneva inquired, "in your opposition to blacks who gain enhanced standing by telling white people what they want to hear about blacks, and those like Minister Farrakhan who gain, if not standing, a kind of notoriety by telling whites what they least want to hear?"

"A good point," I conceded, "but I think the statements by Louis Farrakhan and other outspoken black militants are bold, impolitic, and sometimes outrageous precisely because they are intended for those blacks whose perilous condition places them beyond the courteous, the politic, even the civilities of racial and religious tolerance. These blacks need to hear their rage articulated by those able and willing to do so. They need reassurance that others, not they, are the cause of the wretched circumstances in which they live. Professor Lucius Barker makes this point when, while noting the large differences between whites and blacks regarding attitudes toward Farrakhan, he warns: 'Sooner or later whites must understand that this type of rhetoric and behavior has been fostered by their own ongoing maltreatment of blacks in the American political-social order. As long as such conditions exist, blacks understandably find themselves more receptive to many types of rhetoric and promises of deliverance than would otherwise by the case.'"[31]

"The real paradox here," said Geneva, "is that while whites fear spokespersons like Minister Farrakhan, the risk posed by the Farrakhans in this country is as nothing compared with the risks to all arising from the conditions against which those Farrakhans rail in uncompromising terms."

"I have not talked to him, Geneva, but I rather imagine that Minister Farrakhan understands the rules of racial standing. He knows that abstract condemnation of racism and poverty and the devastation of our communities is inadequate and ineffective. He has decided that the only way to be heard over the racial-standing barrier is to place the blame for racism where it belongs. Using direct, blunt, even abrasive language, he forthrightly charges with evil those who do evil under the racial structure that protects them and persecutes us, that uplifts them regardless of merit and downgrades us regardless of worth."

Looking again at the final page of the text, I remembered the voice's warning that every gift has a price—a price confirmed in the Fifth Rule.

FIFTH RULE

True awareness requires an understanding of the Rules of Racial Standing. As an individual's understanding of these rules increases, there will be more and more instances where one can discern their workings. Using this knowledge, one gains the gift of prophecy about racism, its essence, its goals, even its remedies. The price of this knowledge is the frustration that follows recognition that no amount of public prophecy, no matter its accuracy, can either repeal the Rules of Racial Standing or prevent their operation.

I read the Fifth Rule, read it again, and then looked up at Geneva. "One more dilemma confronting black people and their leaders," I observed.

"It is that," Geneva agreed, "but notice that it reinforces rather than contradicts the admonition on the mountaintop computer screen: 'SPEAK UP, IKE, AN 'SPRESS YO'SE'F!'"

CHAPTER 7

A Law Professor's Protest

Through many dangers, toils, and snares,
I have already come;
'Twas grace that brought me safe thus far,
and grace will lead me home.

—John Newton

E VERYONE IN THE CAMBRIDGE COMMUNITY KNEW IT WAS A disaster at the very moment it happened. In later years, residents would recount the event with the preciseness appropriate to great tragedy: three o'clock on a sunny Saturday afternoon in late fall. None who heard or saw it ever forgot the earth-shaking explosion and the huge, nuclear-like fireball. When the smoke cleared the following day, the former president's residence, 17 Quincy Street, had disappeared. A deep, smoldering crater marked the site on the perimeter of Harvard Yard where the impressive colonial house had stood.

In the explosion and the subsequent inferno, the president of Harvard and one hundred and ninety-six black professors and administrators—the university's total complement of black full-time professionals—died. As part of a year-long campaign to increase minority faculty and staff on campus, the Association of Harvard Black Faculty and Administrators had called for an all-day meeting with Harvard's president. He accepted the Association's invitation, and the meeting had begun as scheduled. A university photographer had stopped in during the lunch break and taken a group photograph. Intended to provide a record of those who attended, it served to confirm those who died.

There were no clues to what or who had caused the explosion, a fact that encouraged endless speculation. Every possibility was explored: accident, terrorism, even supernatural forces. The official investigation, after months of searching, found little more than everyone knew in the first hour after the explosion. A building and all within it had disappeared in a flash of fire that reduced even stone and steel to a fine volcanic ash.

In the absence of answers, surmise served as substitute for fact. Many whites assumed the Association was responsible: that frustrated with their inability to increase their numbers, the blacks—or some of them—had conspired to blow up the meeting place in a bizarre murder-suicide pact. Acting on this theory, racist hate groups launched random attacks on blacks. For their part, blacks were convinced that the tragedy was the work of ultraconservatives, possibly acting with government support. Rumors ignited riots in the inner cities.

The victims became martyrs to the cause of racial equality. The tragedy plus the racial violence, with its threat to the social order, prompted long-dormant government agencies to renew the enforcement of affirmative action. Civil rights groups organized protest marches. In the most spectacular of these, more than a million college students walked from their campuses to Harvard for the massive memorial service held at the Harvard stadium and the surrounding grounds. The investigation did uncover information about what came to be known as the "final meeting."

Though the final meeting at the Quincy Street house was closed, files from both the president's office and the offices of the Association's co-chairmen contained the meeting agenda, statistics detailing what everyone knew: that most schools within the university had no more than one or two black faculty members, and many none at all. The Association had also prepared a report to the president on affirmative action at Harvard, a report dedicated to Dr. W. E. B. Du Bois, who, following his graduation from Fisk University, entered Harvard in the fall of 1888. Two years later, he graduated, cum laude, with a major in philosophy. He was one of five graduating students chosen to speak at the commencement exercises.

In the prologue to its report, the Association noted that Dr. Du Bois would now find that about 10 percent of Harvard's undergraduate students are black. Most contemporary black students, though spared the overt hostility that barred Du Bois from every social activity except the Philosophy Club, do encounter color-based discrimination in many subtle and debilitating forms, and suffer slights and disparaging assumptions about their abilities no less hurtful than those Du Bois endured.

And then there was the problem of faculty and administrators. The statistics were deplorable. According to Harvard's Affirmative Action Plan, during the 1988–89 school year only 15 of the 957 tenured faculty (1.6 percent) were black. And there were only 26 blacks (1.1 percent) among the 2,265 tenure-line faculty position[1] Citing these figures— fairly typical for most colleges and universities[2]—the Association posed the question that underlay both their report and the meeting: How can those of us chosen to pioneer a new era of racial diversity in those previously all-white

---

* The Plan also reports that the university has 1,073 "Academic Managers," of whom 42 are black. There are 37 black executives, administrators, and managers among the 442 employees in this (EAM) category, and 76 blacks of 1,690 persons in the "other" professional classification. The data has changed little since this 1988 report was published.[2]

** Law schools usually have the best minority statistics on the campuses where they are located. But a 1988 study found that about one third of all law schools have no black faculty members. Another third have just one. Less than a tenth have more than three. As to other minorities, the Hispanic proportion of majority-run faculties went from 0.5 percent to 1.0 percent, and the proportion of other minorities from 0.5 percent to 1.0 percent. The study's director, Professor Richard H. Chused, reported that the data "demonstrate that minority professors in general, and black professors in particular, tend to be tokens if they are present at all; that very few majority-run schools have significant numbers of minority teachers; and that minority teachers leave their schools at higher rates than do their white colleagues."[3]

colleges and universities convey our strong sense of betrayal? After two decades of substantial effort to prove ourselves and make a way for others, we fear that the schools that hired us wanted, not committed pioneers, but compliant placebos. Our presence was intended to placate protestors whose threats—made in the late 1960s and early 1970s— are no longer heard or, if heard, are no longer threatening. Now, as then, our institutions relent, on occasion, to student protests and hire a black or some other nonwhite minority teacher with traditional qualifications, preferably one with conservative leanings on racial issues; but that is no progress. It is simply the formalizing of a black tokenism policy: "Hire one if you must, but only one."

Embarrassed and deeply concerned about their minuscule representation on the nation's most prestigious campus, the Association warned that unless Harvard exerted special efforts, contemporary students at Harvard would have access to or contact with only a few more black faculty and administrators than were available to Dr. Du Bois—who had none. Thus, the Association noted that, despite the university's commitment, implementation was seriously deficient. "We must ask why the improved citizenship status of blacks in the last three decades has not wrought concomitant reform in the once all-white status of Harvard's faculty and administrators? What hidden barriers limit the success of so many seemingly well-intentioned affirmative action pledges and programs?"

There were no records of the discussions that followed the opening statements. Investigators, piecing together information gained from files and interviews with victims' relatives and friends, were able to provide a likely summary of what was said. The academic deans, for example, had given Association members varying reasons for the few blacks on their faculties. The decrease in the number of black American doctorates,* the lack or inadequacy of pools from which black applicants might be drawn,** the lack of openings, the lack of funds for hiring new faculty, and the difficulty in obtaining tenure—all were recurring themes during the discussions. The most frequent explanation was that faculty openings required qualifications that few, if any, blacks hold. The deans were less clear in explaining the paucity of black administrators, despite the admittedly larger pool of clearly qualified candidates for these positions.

Judging by earlier meetings, Association members concluded that the academic deans were concerned about minority hiring but comfortable with existing hiring criteria that rely heavily on high grades, preferably earned at prestigious schools. At the final meeting, the Association saw its task as getting the president to recognize that the deans' frequently expressed resistance to hiring African Americans with other than traditional academic backgrounds, regardless of the latter's success and experience in their fields,

---

* The number of blacks receiving doctorates has declined by 26 percent over the past decade, from 1,116 to 820; 50 percent of those earning the doctoral degree at Harvard were in fields other than the arts and sciences. And the number of blacks seeking the masters in education has dropped by 70 percent in recent years.[4]

** As a result of an analysis of minority faculty at several schools of government, an official of the school concluded that availability was the major obstacle confronting the Kennedy School of Government and comparable institutions.

contradicted campus experience in hiring both whites and blacks. They planned to make two points:

1. African Americans have been hired and promoted at Harvard despite (for some) their lack of traditional qualifications. The fact that many of these men and women are now highly effective teachers and productive scholars has done nothing to alter the attitudes of those who doubt that minority candidates without traditional qualifications can succeed.

2. A significant number of whites hired and tenured according to traditional academic criteria do not perform at consistently high levels as teachers and scholars.

Therefore, the Association reasoned, reliance on traditional qualifications served to exclude potentially fine black professors but did not prevent the hiring of whites who proved mediocre teachers and unimpressive scholars.

One month after the explosion and just prior to the massive memorial service to honor all those who lost their lives in the Quincy Street house explosion, a proposal was found among the late president's papers. There were some indications that he had planned to present the paper to the Association at some point during the final meeting. It read:

> I agree that it is time to honor our words with deeds, and
> linking a new affirmative action program with Dr. Du Bois'

name is an excellent idea. In an essay that appeared in 1903, only several months after the publication of *The Souls of Black Folk*, Dr. Du Bois wrote: "The Negro race, like all races, is going to be saved by its exceptional men. The problem of education, then, among Negroes must first of all deal with the *Talented Tenth;* it is the problem of developing the Best of this race that they may guide the Mass away from the contamination and death of the Worst, in their own and other races."[5]

In keeping with Dr. Du Bois' vision, I plan to issue a proclamation that, in commemoration of the centennial of his coming to Harvard, will inaugurate the Du Bois Talented Tenth black faculty recruitment and hiring program. The goal of this program is that by the earliest possible time, ten percent of Harvard's faculty and administrators should be black, Hispanic, or native American men and women.

Our black students need teachers. Teachers are models as well as trainers; and while, as Du Bois and dozens of educational studies would agree, not all teachers of black students need be black, for a healthy and effective learning environment—for whites as well as blacks—some representative number of faculty should be persons of color. Adopting Du Bois' Talented Tenth standard as the immediate goal for all Harvard faculty and administrative positions is both a reasonable and an appropriate means of moving Harvard's affirmative action commitment beyond tokenism.

There were several blank pages in the president's notes where he likely intended to spell out how his plan should be implemented. His closing comment was, though, sufficient to provide his successors with all the direction they needed in that time of shock, mourning, and commitment.

I am proposing a program both worthy of Harvard and capable of exciting enthusiasm and emulation by colleges across the land. Race has served for three centuries as an absolute bar for faculty status at Harvard. It remains the cause of suspicion rather than an opportunity for inclusion and broadening the scope of scholarly inquiry. We must confront and remove these unspoken but no less serious barriers.

My proposal responds to the need for reform that will improve rather than degrade Harvard's standards of scholarly excellence: first, by vigorous effort, vacancies can be filled by blacks who have either traditional qualifications or their equivalent; and, second, where such persons cannot be found or recruited, funding equal to the salaries of those positions will be devoted to fellowships and other support that will enable promising students of color to gain the necessary credentials and experience to fill teaching and staff positions in the future, either here or at another school.

The president's plan, read at the memorial service, electrified the Harvard community. With rare unanimity, it made implementation of the Talented Tenth program a matter of the highest priority. By the following year, the percentage of black and Hispanic faculty and staff reached levels double those at the time of the fatal explosion. In addition, scores of black graduate students were benefiting from the fellowship funds provided in unfilled minority positions. The reform had captured national attention and was being emulated at colleges and universities across the country.

Finally, exactly two years after the never-explained explosion, an elegant building, the new home of the Du Bois Institute, was opened on the site of the disaster—a fitting memorial to the past and a stately witness to the university's ability to merge its commitment to affirmative action with that impressive past.

Who can doubt that so great a disaster—and the concomitant threat of widespread racial disorders—would motivate concerted action to memorialize its victims? Such a memorial would be neither illegal nor wrong. Acceptance of that role without the motivation of grief and the need to memorialize lost colleagues would not render that role less worthy. Indeed, while adding to the luster of a great university, it might well spark a national movement toward closing the gap between the commitment to diversity in academe and the solid action needed to give life to that commitment.

"WELL," GENEVA SAID, as I finished the story, "even if I agree that the humanizing effect of a great disaster can lower white resistance to some racial reform, I don't see what you hoped to accomplish by making that point the heart of your Affirmative Action Report, which, as I understand it, you and the Association of Black Faculty and Administrators actually gave to the president and then, in October 1988, released to the public."*

"Remember," I reminded her, "the black faculty and staff at Harvard had gathered data on affirmative action there and conducted a series of individual meetings with the academic deans of each school. By placing the results of our survey and the interviews with deans in the context of an interesting, albeit fictional story, we hoped to spur debate that would lead to action."

Geneva stared at me. "You must be kidding! Surely, you did not seriously believe that by placing your study of Harvard's affirmative action inadequacies in an allegorical tragedy, you would actually shame those high-level white folks into aggressively doing now what you suggest—and I agree—they might do if the Harvard community suffered a calamity like that portrayed in the story? You, friend, are an optimist!"

"After twenty years at Harvard," I said as emphatically as I could, "an optimist is what I am not! I did hope, though, that our report might stimulate those on campus who support a more diverse faculty to pressure deans and other policy makers. You'll notice we didn't directly condemn either the president or the deans. We wanted to lessen their opposition

---

* The Final Affirmative Action Report received significant press coverage: "Harvard Blacks Make Unusual Plea on Hiring," *New York Times,* 30 October 1988, p. 27; Joanne Ball, "Report Urges More Blacks on Faculty at Harvard," *Boston Globe,* 25 October 1988, p. 17; "Harvard Urged to Hire More Black Educators," *Boston Herald,* 25 October 1988, p. 1; Badiuzzaman Khasru, "Harvard Hiring Is Criticized," *Bay State Banner,* 3 November 1988, p. 1; *Chronicle of Higher Education,* 2 November 1988, p. A14, col. 3. It was also covered in Harvard campus newspapers: see, for example, "Affirmative Action Goals Spur Debate," *Harvard Crimson,* 26 October 1988, p. 1; "Report Calls For Minority Increase," *Harvard University Gazette,* 28 October 1988, p. 1.

and perhaps garner their support for a more vigorous minority hiring program, which would benefit the university as much if not more than the persons of color for whom it was aimed. Basically, though, I wanted to keep the study from suffering the 'released, reported, and quickly forgotten' fate of most race relations reports."

"About the only way you could have done that," Geneva said wryly, as she pointed to the manuscript of my chapter on racial standing, "is have the black faculty and staff publish a report condemning affirmative action policies and urging the university to hire and promote strictly on merit—merit as defined by them, of course."

"Actually," I admitted, "I think some members of our group would have been happier with a report criticizing affirmative action. It was a struggle gaining majority approval for the one we published. Although I'd expected some of our members would have been a little nervous about its unorthodox character, the amount of opposition really surprised me. Black people working at Harvard are particularly anxious to play by the book. They haven't gotten where they are by radical or nonconforming behavior."*

---

* The need for caution was confirmed when Lawrence Watson, the co-chair of the Association, was dismissed from his position as associate dean of the Harvard Graduate School of Design at the end of the school year following publication of the Affirmative Action Report. "Budgetary reasons" were given as the reason for his dismissal, an explanation Watson successfully challenged under the university's administrative procedures. Paradoxically, it was Watson who convinced a majority of the Association—most of whom were nontenured administrators—to support the report on the grounds that they should do no less than he, who was supporting it even though he was a nontenured administrator.

"So, what happened when you released the report? No," Geneva interrupted her question, "let me guess. You received some press coverage—though any untoward happening at all at Harvard is enough to pique media interest. Let's see," she continued, "you must have received a few telephone calls and notes from white liberals commending your report, but I would bet that few of them did anything publicly given the fact that the report—whether or not you intended it as such—was critical of Harvard's progress and condemned as cynical its unwillingness to act unless propelled by a major tragedy."

"Very few campus critics bothered or, I should say, dared to convey their upset to me," I said. "They view my activism as craziness that might make face-to-face criticism dangerous. It's not true, of course. I learned, though, that some of the faculty felt my use of so grisly a story to provoke discussion was unorthodox—in being, I assume, emotional rather than analytical and in seeking to pressure rather than reason with them."

"Did they have a point?" Geneva asked in a chiding tone.

"Perhaps—had I and others not been analyzing the issue to death for months and reasoning ourselves silly without getting any response beyond the usual platitudes, the same old expressions of concern."

"How about the academic deans? After all, it was the meetings with them that formed the basis of your report."

"With a few exceptions, the response of the deans with whom we met was private distress that we publicized the report and public silence regarding our findings. We learned—again, secondhand—that most deans were 'turned off' by the report. In their view, our tactics—so much a departure from the 'old boy' tradition—served as proof that our Association was not serious about improving minority hiring. In what was likely a retaliatory pressure tactic, some officials predicted that our report would harm rather than help minority hiring efforts on the campus. In the same vein, others reportedly were angered that the report questioned their commitment to affirmative action."

"I am certain," Geneva interjected, "that a goodly number of whites in that élite community dismissed as totally unrealistic your report's recommendation that Harvard move aggressively toward a goal of ten-percent black and other previously disadvantaged minority faculty and staff. And I would also bet," she added with a smile, "that more than a few traditional Harvard professors viewed your unorthodox report as the best possible argument why the university should abandon rather than accelerate its affirmative action programs."

"All your conjecture is accurate," I acknowledged sadly. "In effect, Geneva, you're suggesting—none too subtly— that the report may have undermined affirmative action programs as much as if it had called on the university to drop them?"

"Let's just say you probably changed few minds about the worth of affirmative action."

"It's frustrating! What do we have to *do*?" I wondered. "During our meetings with them, I asked some of the deans to imagine the racial statistics—and the power relationships—reversed, with ninety-eight percent of Harvard's faculty and professional staff remaining black more than two decades after a commitment to hire and promote whites. What action, then, would whites take? How to convey the frustration and sense of shame that their presence, the result of earlier protest activity, serves to legitimize hiring policies that remain essentially unchanged?"

"But don't you see?" Geneva exclaimed. "That was a rhetorical question. However helpful in a debate, such a possibility is so totally remote from élite white men's minds that likely no answer even surfaced."

"Most simply looked at me blankly," I recalled. "You know, Geneva, when I agreed to become Harvard's first black faculty member back in 1969, I did so on the express commitment that I was to be the first, but not the last, black hired. I was to be the pioneer, the trailblazer. And, Lord knows, there was plenty of underbrush to clear away—all of it steeped in tradition designed to make it easy for smart young white men from privileged backgrounds, and impossible for everyone else. To look back now, after more than twenty years of clearing the trail and see it all grown over—well, it's a feeling not easy to describe."

"Your metaphors evoke sympathy without providing much enlightenment, friend. What *are* the specific barriers that keep blacks from academic positions?"

"I know the law teaching field best, of course," I replied cautiously, "but, as the Association discovered in putting together its report, the barriers are complex, interwoven, and infinitely flexible. We identified several strands of resistance: white superiority, faculty conservatism, scholarly conformity, and tokenism.

"The Harvard administration would deem deeply insulting any suggestion that white superiority was a current barrier to hiring blacks. But the fact is that for more than two hundred years before Du Bois' years at Harvard—and likely for three quarters of this century—the strictures of law and widely held prejudices about the superiority of whites and the inferiority of blacks barred *all* blacks—including any with Du Bois' academic qualifications—from any teaching or administrative positions. The inertia sustained during this long exclusion period was not eliminated by antidiscrimination laws. Standards of qualification now subtly play the role once performed overtly by policies of racial exclusion.

"Actually, tenure may be a more important barrier than overt racism, though the two are clearly linked. Tenured faculty are principally responsible for hiring and promotion decisions. Almost by definition, they're conservative when it comes to admitting new members to their ranks. They take seriously their roles as guardians of Harvard's scholarly reputation—a guardianship not evil in itself, but in practice it simply replicates the status quo by selecting candidates from similar backgrounds, with interests and ideology like those of current faculty members. It may be my racial paranoia, but I sense that the way a faculty candidate will "fit in" receives great—if unacknowledged—weight in many faculty hiring and promotion decisions. This insider bias 'for those like us,' likely to eliminate many white candidates, is almost sure to exclude most black ones."*

I went on to discuss an issue in which I was deeply concerned. Even outstanding scholarship can, if performed in a nontraditional format, disqualify a candidate seeking a position or promotion. Narrow measures of excellence harm many candidates, but tend to exclude disproportionately blacks and other people of color whose approach, voice, or conclusions may depart radically from the usual forms. Minority faculty whose research is oriented toward political or practical issues are often dismissed as having introduced ideological concerns into scholarship. As a result, the selection process favors blacks who reject or minimize their blackness, exhibit little empathy for or interest in black students, and express views on racial issues far removed from positions

---

* My concerns about "insider preference" are shared by the University of Massachusetts philosophy professor Robert Paul Wolff, who wrote me following the release of the Association's report, warning that we should not "allow Harvard to get away with the myth that it searches the world for the best possible people. . . . The fact of the matter is that the appointment of a dozen solid, productive, interesting black academics would raise the general level of competence at Harvard." Professor Wolff, a Harvard undergraduate, graduate student, and instructor in philosophy and general education, said:

> We are asked, over and over, to believe that Harvard's Olympian commitment to outstanding quality is at war with its noble condescension to the moral demands of affirmative action. [Challenging this stance and suggesting that the faculties in several departments pass over promising junior faculty to hire nonthreatening and undistinguished persons, he warns] The elevated standards which Harvard so prides itself on only come into play when a woman or a black is a candidate. Then, suddenly, the question becomes: is this the best person in the entire galaxy, regardless of age, language, or even species?[6]

held by most blacks including—often enough—the student groups who urge the hiring of more minority teachers.

"I realize that this gets into the subjective area of evaluating the quality and worth of scholarship. The faculty are understandably concerned about what they might define as a 'politicizing of scholarship,' but they should not condemn scholarship that has a political dimension—that is, a perspective different from their own. In addition, the evaluation process should include criteria for valuing a person's practical orientation, rather than automatically concluding that such interests are 'soft' or 'unscientific.' Professor Mari Matsuda has, in discussing the academic value of a more integrated legal landscape, argued that new voices will emphasize difference, and thus give new vigor to theoretical debate. An outsider's experience of discrimination or poverty may, for example, though differing from textbook cases, be valid knowledge, both concrete and personal: 'To the extent legal discourse is distillable into conflicts over distribution of resources, the voice of the poor will force us to discuss such conflicts with full awareness of the reality of American poverty.'[7]

"Finally, there's the barrier of tokenism. While the lack of an adequate pool of blacks with traditional qualifications serves as the major excuse for little or no progress, the drop in interest in minority recruitment after one or two blacks are hired demonstrates that there is an unconscious but no less real ceiling on the number óf blacks who will be hired in a given department—regardless of their qualifications."

"A daunting list of barriers," Geneva remarked, "but even many black academics would not agree with every item and,

as you admit, would certainly not agree that your various protests are an effective means to improve minority hiring. The
fact is, friend, any number of blacks are more than willing
to play the token role at Harvard and other major schools.
Some of them will feel better, more 'legitimate,' if there is only
one of them. They believe as well that, by quietly doing their
jobs, they better serve those students whose protests got them
hired. They likely see you as a disruptive force, always bringing up racial issues and making it hard for them and the school
to view black faculty as 'just faculty.' Whites who set policy at
these institutions know this. You should not deny it."

"You're right, of course," I acknowledged wearily. "Some
of these young blacks with degrees from prestigious schools
I didn't know existed when I was young, assume they were
hired solely because they are good. Race, for them, is irrel-
evant. What they overlook are all those who struggled and
risked so that they, the young blacks, would not—unlike the
generations of no less able blacks who preceded them—be
rejected for racial reasons.

"I think it is damned sad, but they are not *me!* I haven't
forgotten the students whose protests, at the risk of expul-
sion, led to my being hired. I don't think I ever told you,
Geneva, but back in the mid-1960s, I applied for a teaching
position at Harvard not once, but twice. The school's summary rejections turned into vigorous recruitment in 1969,
after students mounted protests about the time of the riots
that followed Martin Luther King's assassination.

"Of course," I added, "I'm not seeking sympathy. With
all my problems with my faculty colleagues, I think law

teaching is the best job in the world. Moreover, some black and white faculty support my protest efforts."

"Right. But isn't it usually quietly and from a distance? That was certainly true with your decision in 1990 to take a leave without pay to protest Harvard's failure to hire and tenure a woman of color. Nor was it any less true in 1986 when you protested the faculty's denial of tenure to a white woman who was rejected, you felt, because of her connection with critical legal studies, a form of jurisprudence not particularly popular with many faculty members. Oh, and lest I forget, didn't you also resign your deanship at the University of Oregon Law School in 1985 to protest that faculty's failure to offer a position to an Asian-American applicant?"

"I did what I felt was appropriate and within my power to protest injustices after analysis and reasoning failed to convince my colleagues they were wrong. No one has to tell me how deeply invested law teachers are in their stellar grades and law review editorship standards. Even so, I keep trying new ways to make them see what they clearly do not want to see, what perhaps they're incapable of seeing. And not only at Harvard, I use these arguments at law schools across the country.

"For example, the difficulty many teachers have in evaluating nontraditional scholarship is rather like the resistance composers of modern music encounter with audiences committed to the standard repertoire of Brahms, Beethoven, Haydn, and Mozart. My early experience with classical music was with two relatively modern works: Igor Stravinsky's

The Rite of Spring and Paul Hindemith's *Mathis de Maler*. With my ear attuned to works of this genre, it was difficult for me to understand why so much of the concert-going public preferred and, indeed, demanded, the old masters. I came to recognize that the initial introduction to an art form, as to one's native language, creates a strong preference for that mode. Other styles can seem dissonant and unmusical—inaccessible without considerable effort.

"What I have noted about music is applicable to every form of literature and art. The presentation of truth in new forms provokes resistance, confounding those committed to accepted measures for determining the quality and validity of statements made and conclusions reached, and making it difficult for them to respond and adjudge what is acceptable. We are, the literary critic Terry Eagleton reminds us, so attached to what we consider the aesthetically pleasing and cohesive whole of social life, that the 'socially disruptive, by contrast, is as instantly offensive as a foul smell.'[8] The 'offensiveness response' is, I suggest, particularly likely when the innovators have backgrounds and outlooks greatly different from those who have the responsibility to judge."

"It's an argument," Geneva observed, "that is easier to understand than accept. You are dealing with professors for whom your facts and experience-based arguments are incomprehensible, not convincing. How can you expect them to accept your views on faith when by their standards, the structure of the writing reveals serious deviation from the faith most legal scholars have placed in doctrinal exegesis?"

"Aha, Ms. Crenshaw!" I responded. "It's clear that you could hold your own in any law school's obfuscatory discourse. But, to be serious, I believe that however hard it is, these people must stretch their comprehension to embrace these nontraditional writings, from which I and many others have learned much about the law and how it functions in our society. If the purpose of scholarly writing is to communicate ideas, to blaze new intellectual trails that broaden the basis for serious debate, then even nontraditional scholars can become productive and deserve serious consideration for hiring and tenure at any school."

"That's all well and good, friend—but I can hear them now asking you what does *productive* mean in legal scholarship? How does it translate into a justification for bestowing a tenured position on someone who lacks those credentials they view as the foundation stone of their law school's reputation?"

I took a deep breath, feeling as though Geneva was taking almost too seriously her role as devil's advocate. "I can't claim objectivity, Geneva, but I and many other minority legal scholars—for example Robert Williams, Angela Harris, Kimberlè Crenshaw, Mari Matsuda, Jerome Culp, Richard Delgado, Gerald Torres, Lani Gunier, and Charles Lawrence[9]—have borrowed from other disciplines like philosophy, literary criticism, and the social sciences. With what some of us are calling critical race theory, we are attempting to sing a new scholarly song—even if to some listeners our style is strange, our lyrics unseemly."

"Why do you do it," Geneva asked me sadly, "given the predictable resistance, the almost certain rejection?"

I shook my head. "As I told you at the outset, Geneva, it's something about being a lawyer and having the feeling that you can convince reasonable people that your point of view is correct. And, of course, I truly believe that analysis of legal developments through fiction, personal experience, and the stories of people on the bottom illustrates how race and racism continue to dominate our society. The techniques also help in assessing sexism, classism, homophobia, and other forms of oppression. In fact, a good deal of the writing in critical race theory stresses that oppressions are neither neatly divorceable from one another nor amenable to strict categorization."[10]

Geneva nodded, but wondered whether we might get so engrossed in our critical race theory ideology that we lost contact with real world problems. I acknowledged the danger, but reassured her that we think it as important to reform the standards for hiring law teachers and evaluating their work—white men as well as minorities and white women—as to change admissions practices that until a few decades ago barred all but a few black people from gaining admission to law schools. Unfortunately, although most law teachers agree that our classrooms are better and more viable and lively places for learning because of the diversity of our student bodies, far, far fewer share our view that more diversity on law faculties would lead to equally impressive improvements in the law school community.

"Geneva, the legal profession is a mess. Polls show that a high percentage of lawyers are unhappy with their work.[11] Dishonesty is, if not rampant, sufficiently high to cause concern.[12] Although legal education is not the cause of all these problems, it is increasingly obvious to some of us that staffing faculties with people who earned high grades and have, for the most part, never practiced, may be one way of training more law teachers with similar credentials, but it does not produce lawyers able to practice effectively and have satisfying experiences in the modern world.

"No," I assured her, "for us, this writing is not some idle vogue. Nor are we willfully confrontational. Rather, we feel we must understand so as better to oppose the dire forces that are literally destroying the many people who share our racial heritage."

I went on to tell Geneva how I and other minority teachers are encouraged, even inspired in our scholarly pioneering by the Old Testament's reminder that neither the challenge we face nor its difficulty are new. Indeed, no fewer than three psalms begin by urging "O sing unto the Lord a new song";[13] as does Isaiah, who admonishes: "Sing to the Lord a new song, his praise from the end of the earth!"[14]

"No, Geneva," I went on, "we do not expect praise for our legal scholarship that departs from the traditional. We simply seek understanding and that tolerance without which no new songs will ever be heard."

CHAPTER 8

Racism's Secret Bonding

And Moses stretched forth his rod toward heaven:
and the LORD sent thunder and hail, . . . And the
hail smote throughout all the land of Egypt all that
was in the field, . . . Only in the land of Goshen,
where the children of Israel were, was there no
hail. . . . And when Pharaoh saw that the rain and
the hail and the thunders were ceased, . . . the heart
of Pharaoh was hardened, neither would he let the
children of Israel go.

—Exodus 9:23–35

THE FIRST OF WHAT CAME TO BE KNOWN AS THE RACIAL
Data Storms fell on the Fourth of July. Setting the pattern for the storms that followed, it broke exactly at noon
and lasted for precisely a half hour. Over the vast expanse
of fifty states, including Alaska and Hawaii, skies darkened
quickly, turning bright day into eerie twilight. Lightning
bolts pierced the gloom and were particularly frightening

because they slithered almost vertically from sky to earth. Each lightning flash was followed by a cannonlike crack of thunder. No rain fell. Instead, there was a precipitation of visible, though quite thin slivers of hitherto-unknown energy rays. These rays did not soak people's clothing and skin but—easily penetrating umbrellas, raincoats, even the stoutest structures—entered their consciousness and flooded them with data.

Then the real fear set in. There was no need to read about the Data Storm or watch it on television. Every U.S. citizen could report from personal experience that the July Fourth storm rained down statistical data about the number of Africans who had been captured, brought to these shores, and enslaved during the years of the slave trade. Those newly soaked not only knew the statistics but experienced the horrified feelings of the subjects of those statistics. As a kind of rhetorical counterpoint to the statistical bombardment, there rang in the ears of the white Americans undergoing the data deluge the famous antislavery speech Frederick Douglass presented on the Fourth of July, 1852.

> What, to the American slave, is your 4th of July? I answer; a day that reveals to him, more than all other days in the year, the gross injustice and cruelty to which he is the constant victim. To him, your celebration is a sham; your boasted liberty, an unholy license; your national greatness, swelling vanity; your sounds of rejoicing are empty, all heartless; your denunciation of tyrants, brass fronted impudence; your shouts of liberty and equality, hollow mockery; your

prayers and hymns, your sermons and thanksgivings, with all your religious parade and solemnity, are, to Him, mere bombast, fraud, deception, impiety, and hypocrisy—a thin veil to cover up crimes which would disgrace a nation of savages. There is not a nation on the earth guilty of practices more shocking and bloody than are the people of the United States, at this very hour.[1]

Recovering that evening, government officials promised their shaken constituents to leave no stone unturned in getting to the bottom of the phenomenon. In the meantime, they tried to dismiss it as a Fourth of July prank that was neither funny nor patriotic. "It will not happen again," scientists assured citizens, but this prediction could not support any explanation of how the data deluge occurred in the first place. There was one major clue to its cause. African Americans had not been deluged, had not even noticed the storm. When they learned what had happened, blacks spontaneously reached a single conclusion. "Guess," they asked one another, "who is going to get the blame for this?"

The next day, the Racial Data Storm returned. Amidst awesome thunder and lightning, the deluge rained down statistics on black unemployment and the consistently large disparities (averaging two and one half times) between jobless figures for blacks and whites. The figures, while astonishing, were not new. The data contained as well, though, the feelings of frustration, despair, and rage that blacks experience when discrimination bars them from jobs they would otherwise obtain. These data-related feelings were unnerving even to unemployed whites. The more predictable feeling so evident after the first storm—outrage—was wholly absent. In part, the deluge itself seemed less invasive, as though the waves had been fine-tuned to convey their messages with a minimum of disruption.

In the days that followed, the storms and their accompanying background lectures continued. The data continued to convey information and evoke feelings about disparities—in comparison with whites—in infant death rates, educational attainment, income based on education, life expectancies, prison terms for the same crime, the death sentence, and housing and health care costs and availability.

After a few weeks, complaints that government "do something" about the daily deluges diminished—as ever more people demanded that government at every level act to address the nation's social ills, including racial injustice, and the heavy financial, political, and moral burden racism imposed on all races. Prompted by business groups who were satisfied with the status quo, elected officials tried to justify delay by saying the primary job was to catch whomever was causing the Racial Data Storms, but the citizens paid no attention. Finally, massive, day-long sitdown strikes, conducted at the workplace and in the middle of busy thoroughfares, persuaded both official and behind-the-scenes powers to act.

There was further impetus for reform after the first few states to initiate broad social reforms reported that the Data Storms had stopped and been replaced by moderate rains that fell each night from 2:00 to 4:00 A.M. The reforms included new legislative efforts to protect against discrimination based on race, sex, religion, sexual orientation, and physical challenge, along with the means to enforce them vigorously. But it turned out that far less enforcement was required. The daily doses of feeling what discrimination is really like had made many white people eager to comply with the new laws.

Finally, government intelligence agents located the source of the Racial Data Storms. On the morning when they planned to enter the secluded scientific site high in the Rocky Mountains, the chief suspects—three black scientists— managed to stow away on a space shuttle and, after take- off, hijacked it. At a point high in the shuttle's orbit, they exited through the shuttle's cargo doors and disappeared into the black of space—whether to attempt a re-entry into the Earth's atmosphere or to head for another planet no one ever learned. There was no doubt, however, that they had left behind them the greatest social reform movement America had ever known.

———

"WELL," GENEVA ASKED, "do you think sweeping reforms are possible in the wake of such brilliant manipulation of meteorology, statistics, and psychology?"

"I am far less certain than I was twenty, even ten, years ago," I replied, "that our long-held belief in education is the key to the race problem. You know," and I explained the old formula, "education leads to enlightenment. Enlightenment opens the way to empathy. Empathy foreshadows reform. In other words, that whites—once given a true understanding of the evils of racial discrimination, once able to *feel* how it harms blacks—would find it easy, or easier, to give up racism."

"Yes, that is certainly what we have hoped for," Geneva agreed, "but now you have doubts? Doubts based on——"

"Experience, Geneva, experience. Even older and wiser, it's hard for me to admit, but we fool ourselves when we argue that whites do not know what racial subordination does to its victims. Oh, they may not know the details of the harm, or its scope, but they *know*. Knowing is the key to racism's greatest value to individual whites and to their interest in maintaining the racial status quo."

"Watch it, friend!" Geneva cautioned. "Your civil rights colleagues who consider your giving up on integration to be an abject surrender to racism, will deem blasphemy your loss of faith in the value of educating whites to racism's evils."

"Don't I know it?" I replied sadly, thinking of some of the motivations for racist behavior that we understand, and trying to connect them with other factors, possibly hidden ones we haven't yet considered. We've long known, as I told Geneva, that poor whites prefer to identify with what Professor Kimberlè Crenshaw calls the "dominant circle" of well-to-do whites,[2*] particularly those who attribute social problems to blacks rather than to the policies that they, the upper-class policy makers, have designed and implemented. No less accurate, if more earthy, than Crenshaw's is the novelist Toni Morrison's assessment of how the presence of blacks enables a bonding by whites across a vast

---

* See introduction, page 9.

socioeconomic divide. When asked why blacks and whites can't bridge the abyss in race relations, Morrison replied:

> [B]ecause black people have always been used as a buffer in this country between powers to prevent class war, to prevent other kinds of real conflagrations.
>
> If there were no black people here in this country, it would have been Balkanized. The immigrants would have torn each other's throats out, as they have done everywhere else. But in becoming an American, from Europe, what one has in common with that other immigrant is contempt for *me*—it's nothing else but color. Wherever they were from, they would stand together. They could all say, "I am not *that*." So in that sense, becoming an American is based on an attitude: an exclusion of me.
>
> It wasn't negative to them—it was unifying. When they got off the boat, the second word they learned was "nigger." Ask them—I grew up with them. I remember in the fifth grade a smart little boy who had just arrived and didn't speak any English. He sat next to me. I read well, and I taught him to read just by doing it. I remember the moment he found out that I was black—a nigger. It took him six months; he was told. And that's the moment when he belonged, that was his entrance. Every immigrant knew he would not come at the very bottom. He had to come above at least one group—and that was us.[3]

"You know, Geneva," I mused, "Morrison's observation gains in validity as the Eastern Europeans—freed of the authoritarian domination of Communist control—engage in fierce and bloody ethnic conflicts. Those conflicts, and their violent counterparts in other parts of the world, reveal the role of blacks that enables Americans to boast that this nation is a melting pot of people from many origins."

"I understand," Geneva interrupted. "Americans achieve a measure of social stability through their unspoken pact to keep blacks on the bottom—an aspect of social functioning that more than any other has retained its viability and its value to general stability from the very beginning of the American experience down to the present day. Indeed, as Professor Jennifer Hochschild has recognized, racism is in a state of symbiosis with liberal democracy in this country.[4]* And, if all this is true, does that not mean that we need a truly extraordinary educational campaign, something like a data deluge?"

"So, I would think, but I have the sense that it's an open secret everyone has agreed on, however much individuals may deplore it from time to time. Indeed, I wonder whether the plight of black people in this country isn't caused by factors more fundamental even than white racism, more essential than good government to a civilized society? While some racial reform can be pressured by financial considerations, disaster, threat, guilt, love, and, yes, even education, there may be a primary barrier to the racial reformation which nullifies all these. I wonder, that is, whether—in the melding of millions of individuals into a nation—some within it

---

* See introduction, page 12.

must be sacrificed, killed, or kept in misery so that the rest who share the guilt for this monstrous wrong, can bring out of their guilt those qualities of forbearance and tolerance essential to group survival and growth? And, if so, then who in the legal system plays the more important role—the prosecutors who are the instruments of the sacrifices mandated by a social physics we do not understand, or the defendants whose efforts are destined to fail but who, by those efforts, serve to camouflage the bitter reality of those sacrifices from the society and—alas—from themselves as well?"

As I wound up, Geneva just looked at me blankly, her face reflecting my own stark frame of mind.

"A grim outlook, I know," I said, "and one that has taken on confirming, metaphorical muscle for me in Ursula Le Guin's haunting short story 'The Ones Who Walk Away from Omelas.'"

I went on to give a brief account of the idyllic community in the story, of a prosperous and sophisticated people, much given to carnivals, parades, and festivals of all kinds; their leaders, wise and free of corruption.

"There is in Omelas neither crime nor want. In a word, its people are extremely happy.

"But there is a problem, an open secret. It's a secret that forces some who learn of it—and some who have known it for a long time—to conclude that they cannot remain, and they leave Omelas. They leave and never look back, never return."

Reaching over to my bookshelf, I took down the book of Le Guin's short stories and opened it to the passage that had haunted me since I'd read it some days earlier.

In a basement under one of the beautiful public buildings of Omelas, or perhaps in the cellar of one of its spacious private homes, there is a room. It has one locked door, and no window. A little light seeps in dustily between cracks in the boards, secondhand from a cobwebbed window somewhere across the cellar. . . . The floor is dirt, a little damp to the touch, as cellar dirt usually is. The room is about three paces long and two wide: a mere broom closet or disused tool room. In the room a child is sitting. It might be a boy or a girl. It looks about six, but actually is nearly ten. It is feebleminded. Perhaps it was born defective, or perhaps it has become imbecile through fear, malnutrition, and neglect. . . . The door is always locked, and nobody ever comes, except that sometimes—the child has no understanding of time or interval—sometimes the door rattles terribly and opens, and a person, or several people, are there. One of them may come in and kick the child to make it stand up. The others never come close, but peer in at it with frightened, disgusted eyes. The food bowl and water jug are hastily filled, the door is locked, the eyes disappear. The people at the door never say anything, but the child, who has not always lived in the tool room, and can remember sunlight and its mother's voice, sometimes speaks. "I will be good," it says. "Please let me out. I will be good!" They never answer.

They all know it is there, all the people of Omelas. Some of them have come to see it, others are content merely to know it is there. They all know that it has to be there. Some of them understand why, and some do not,

but they all understand that their happiness, the beauty
of their city, the tenderness of their friendships, the health
of their children, the wisdom of their scholars, the skill
of their makers, even the abundance of their harvest and
the kindly weathers of their skies, depend wholly on this
child's abominable misery.[5]

Geneva sat quietly for a time, absorbed in thought. "A fine
story," she said finally, "and an apt metaphor for the knowing but unspoken alliance whereby all whites are bonded—as
bell hooks says—by racism.[6] And," she added, "as paradox-
ical as it seems, viewing racism as an amalgam of guilt, responsibility, and power—all of which are generally known
but never acknowledged—may explain why educational programs are destined to fail. More important, the onus of this
open but unmentionable secret about racism marks the critical difference between blacks and whites in this country, the
unbreachable barrier, the essence of why blacks can never
be deemed the orthodox, the standard, the conventional. Indeed, the fact that, as victims, we suffer racism's harm but,
as a people, cannot share the responsibility for that harm,
may be the crucial component in a definition of what it is to
be black in America."

"So," I said, "you see why I was impressed but not com-
pletely convinced by your Data Storm allegory. For all the
reasons we have been discussing, being black in America
means we are ever the outsiders. As such, we are expendable
and must live always at risk of some ultimate betrayal by
those who will treat such treachery as a right."

Geneva frowned. "I guess what you say is right, but now that we have expanded—exploded, really—the education-as-cure-for-racism notion, there is something more. Toni Morrison, you know, is not the only witness to the fact that learning the term *nigger* made new immigrants from Europe 'feel instantly American.' Why, 'every white immigrant who got off the boat was allowed,' as Andrew Hacker writes, 'to talk about "the niggers" within 10 minutes of landing in America.'[7] Ralph Ellison, too, saw that 'whites could look at the social position of blacks and feel that color formed an easy and reliable gauge for determining to what extent one was or was not an American.' But he saw this as 'tricky magic,' because despite the racial difference and social status, 'something indisputably American about Negroes not only raised doubts about the white man's value system but aroused the troubling suspicion that whatever else the true American is, he is also somehow black.'"[8]

In the essay of Ellison's from which Geneva was quoting, he reviews the long history—fantasy, he calls it—of an America free of blacks. He calls it an absurd fantasy, one that fascinates blacks no less than whites and that becomes operative whenever the nation grows weary of the struggle toward the ideal of American democratic equality. In arguing that blacks are a unique and essential part of American culture, Ellison contends that without blacks, the nation's economic, political, and cultural history would have been far different. And, because they are an essential component of this country's make-up, he warns that those who would use the removal of blacks as a radical therapy to achieve a national catharsis would destroy rather than cure the patient.

"Do you think," I asked, "that recognition of our essential cultural role may protect us from the ultimate betrayal we both fear?"

"On the contrary," she said firmly, "I believe that the notion that we blacks, the immutable outsiders, might nevertheless be the bearers of the culture, increases our risk dramatically."

"Then, you differ with Ralph Ellison," and I took his book from the shelf. "He concludes his essay by acknowledging that blacks, of the many groups that compose this country, suffered the harsh realities of the human condition. Because of our past fate, 'for blacks, there are no hiding places down here, not in suburbia or in penthouse, neither in country nor in city. They are an American people who are geared to what *is* and who yet are driven by a sense of what is possible for human life to be in this society.' He predicts that the nation could not survive being deprived of blacks' presence because, 'by the irony implicit in the dynamics of American democracy, they symbolize both its most stringent testing and the possibility of its greatest human freedom.'⁹

"Ellison's optimism cannot conceal the additional dimension he provides to the scapegoat theme in Le Guin's story. He is telling—or, rather, reminding—us that black people are not innocent children chosen at random to perform the psychologically necessary role of social cohesion. Rather, they are the nation's conscience, but he says it better than I."

Taking the book from me, Geneva read the passage I pointed to:

> Listen: it is the black American who puts pressure upon the nation to live up to its ideals. It is he who gives creative tension to our struggle for justice and for the elimination of those factors, social and psychological, which make for slums and shaky suburban communities. . . . Without the black American, something irrepressibly hopeful and creative would go out of the American spirit, and the nation might well succumb to the moral slobbism that has ever threatened its existence from within.[10]

"In other words," I suggested when she looked up, "we're a race of Jeremiahs, prophets calling for the nation to repent."

"Exactly!" Geneva said. "And you know what nations do to their prophets?"

"I do. About the least dire fate for a prophet is that one preaches, and no one listens; that one risks all to speak the truth, and nobody cares."

CHAPTER 9

The Space Traders

<hr />

I JANUARY. THE FIRST SURPRISE WAS NOT THEIR ARRIVAL. The radio messages had begun weeks before, announcing that one thousand ships from a star far out in space would land on 1 January 2000, in harbors along the Atlantic coast from Cape Cod to North Carolina. Well before dawn on that day, millions of people across North America had awakened early to witness the moment the ships entered Earth's atmosphere. However expected, to the watchers, children of the electronic age, the spaceships' approach was as awesome as had been that earlier one of three small ships, one October over five hundred years before, to the Indians of the island of Santo Domingo in the Caribbean.[1]

No, the first surprise was the ships themselves. The people who lined the beaches of New Jersey where the first ships were scheduled to arrive, saw not anything NASA might have dreamed up, but huge vessels, the size of aircraft carriers, which the old men in the crowd recognized as being pretty much like the box-shaped landing craft that carried Allied troops to the Normandy beachheads during the Second World War.

As the sun rose on that cold bright morning, the people on the shore, including an anxious delegation of government officials and media reporters, witnessed a fantastic display of eerie lights and strange sound—evidently the visitors' salute to their American hosts. Almost unnoticed during the spectacle, the bow of the leading ship slowly lowered. A sizable party of the visitors—the first beings from outer space anyone on Earth had ever seen—emerged and began moving majestically across the water toward shore. The shock of seeing these beings, regal in appearance and bearing, literally walking on the waves was more thrilling than frightening. At least, no one panicked.

Then came the second surprise. The leaders of this vast armada could speak English. Moreover, they spoke in the familiar comforting tones of former President Reagan, having dubbed his recorded voice into a computerized language-translation system.

After the initial greetings, the leader of the U.S. delegation opened his mouth to read his welcoming speech—only the first of several speeches scheduled to be given on this historic occasion by the leaders of both political parties and other eminent citizens, including—of course—stars of the entertainment and sports worlds. But before he could begin, the principal spokesperson for the space people (and it wasn't possible to know whether it was man or woman or something else entirely) raised a hand and spoke crisply, and to the point.

And this point constituted the third surprise. Those mammoth vessels carried within their holds treasure of which the United States was in most desperate need: gold, to bail out the almost bankrupt federal, state, and local governments; special chemicals capable of unpolluting the environment, which was becoming daily more toxic, and restoring it to the pristine state it had been before Western explorers set foot on it; and a totally safe nuclear engine and fuel, to relieve the nation's all-but-depleted supply of fossil fuel. In return, the visitors wanted only one thing—and that was to take back to their home star all the African Americans who lived in the United States.

The jaw of every one of the welcoming officials dropped, not a word of the many speeches they had prepared suitable for the occasion. As the Americans stood in stupefied silence, the visitors' leader emphasized that the proposed trade was for the Americans freely to accept or not, that no force would be used. Neither then nor subsequently did the leader or any other of the visitors, whom anchorpersons on that evening's news shows immediately labeled the "Space Traders," reveal why they wanted only black people or what plans they had for them should the United States be prepared to part with that or any other group of its citizens. The leader only reiterated to his still-dumbfounded audience that, in exchange for the treasure they had brought, they wanted to take away every American citizen categorized as black on their birth certificate or other official identification. The Space Traders said they would wait sixteen days for a response to their offer. That is, on 17 January—the day when in that year the birthday of Martin Luther King, Jr., was to be observed—they would depart carrying with them every black man, woman, and child in the nation and leave behind untold treasure. Otherwise, the Space Traders' leader shrugged and glanced around—at the oil slick in the water, at the dead gulls on the beach, at the thick shadow of smog that obscured the sky on all but the windiest days. Then the visitors walked back over the waves and returned to their ships.

Their departure galvanized everyone—the delegation, the watchers on the beach, the President glued to his television screen in the White House, citizens black and white throughout the country. The President, who had been advised to stay in the White House out of concern for his security, called Congress into special session and scheduled a cabinet meeting for the next morning. Governors reconvened any state legislatures not already in session. The phones of members of Congress began ringing, as soon as the millions of people viewing the Space Traders' offer on television saw them move back across the water, and never stopped till the morning of 17 January.

There was a definite split in the nature of the calls—a split that reflected distinctly different perceptions of the Space Traders. Most white people were, like the welcoming delegation that morning, relieved and pleased to find the visitors from outer space unthreatening. They were not human, obviously, but resembled the superhuman, good-guy characters in comic books; indeed, they seemed to be practical, no-nonsense folks like regular Americans.

On the other hand, many American blacks—whether watching from the shore or on their television screens—had seen the visitors as distinctly unpleasant, even menacing in appearance. While their perceptions of the visitors differed, black people all agreed that the Space Traders looked like bad news—and their trade offer certainly was—and burned up the phone lines urging black leaders to take action against it.

But whites, long conditioned to discounting any statements of blacks unconfirmed by other whites, chose now, of course, to follow their own perceptions. "Will the blacks never be free of their silly superstitions?" whites asked one another with condescending smiles. "Here, in this truly historic moment, when America has been selected as the site for this planet's first contact with people from another world, the blacks just revert to their primitive fear and foolishness." Thus, the blacks' outrage was discounted in this crisis; they had, as usual, no credibility.

And it *was* a time of crisis. Not only because of the Space Traders' offer per se, but because that offer came when the country was in dire straits. Decades of conservative, laissez-faire capitalism had emptied the coffers of all but a few of the very rich. The nation that had, in the quarter-century after the Second World War, funded the reconstruction of the free world had, in the next quarter-century, given itself over to greed and willful exploitation of its natural resources. Now it was struggling to survive like any third-world nation.

Massive debt had curtailed all but the most necessary services. The environment was in shambles, as reflected by the fact that the sick and elderly had to wear special masks whenever they ventured out-of-doors. In addition, supplies of crude oil and coal were almost exhausted. The Space Traders' offer had come just in time to rescue America. Though few gave voice to their thoughts, many were thinking that the trade offer was, indeed, the ultimate solution to the nation's troubles.

2 JANUARY. THE insomnia that kept the American people tossing and turning that first night of the new century did not spare the White House. As soon as the President heard the Space Traders' post-arrival proposition on television, his political instincts immediately locked into place. This was big! And it looked from the outset like a "no win" situation—not a happy crisis at the start of an election year. Even so, he had framed the outline of his plan by the time his cabinet members gathered at eight o'clock the next morning.

There were no blacks in his cabinet. Four years before, during his first election campaign, the President had made some vague promises of diversity when speaking to minority gatherings. But after the election, he thought, What the hell! Most blacks and Hispanics had not supported him or his party. Although he had followed the practice of keeping one black on the Supreme Court, it had not won him many minority votes. He owed them nothing. Furthermore, the few black figures in the party always seemed to him overly opportunistic and, to be frank, not very smart. But now, as the cabinet members arrived, he wished he had covered his bases better.

In the few hours since the Space Traders' offer, the White House and the Congress had been inundated with phone calls and telegrams. The President was not surprised that a clear majority spontaneously urged acceptance of the offer.

"Easy for them to say," he murmured to an aide. "I'll bet most of those who favor the trade didn't sign or give their names."

"On the contrary," the assistant replied, "the callers are identifying themselves, and the telegrams are signed."

At least a third of the flood of phone calls and faxes urging quick acceptance of the offer expressed the view that what the nation would give up—its African-American citizens—was as worthwhile as what it would receive. The statements accurately reflected relations at the dawn of the new century. The President had, like his predecessors for the last generation, successfully exploited racial fears and hostility in his election campaign. There had been complaints, of course, but those from his political opponents sounded like sour grapes. They, too, had tried to minimize the input of blacks so as not to frighten away white voters.

The race problem had worsened greatly in the 1990s. A relatively small number of blacks had survived the retrogression of civil rights protection, perhaps 20 percent having managed to make good in the increasingly technologically oriented society. But, without anyone acknowledging it and with hardly a peep from the press, more than one half of the group had become outcasts. They were confined to former inner-city areas that had been divorced from their political boundaries. High walls surrounded these areas, and armed guards controlled entrance and exit around the clock. Still, despite all precautions, young blacks escaped from time to time to terrorize whites. Long dead was the dream that this black underclass would ever "overcome."

The President had asked Gleason Golightly, the conservative black economics professor, who was his unofficial black cabinet member, to attend the meeting. Golightly was smart and seemed to be truly conservative, not a man ready to sing any political tune for a price. His mere presence as a person of color at this crucial session would neutralize any possible critics in the media, though not in the black civil rights community.

The cabinet meeting came to order.

"I think we all know the situation," the President said. "Those extraterrestrial beings are carrying in their ships a guarantee that America will conquer its present problems and prosper for at least all of this new century."

"I would venture, sir," the Vice President noted, "that the balance of your term will be known as 'America's Golden Age.' Indeed, the era will almost certainly extend to the terms of your successor."

The President smiled at the remark, as—on cue—did the cabinet. "The VP is right, of course," the President said. "Our visitors from outer space are offering us the chance to correct the excesses of several generations. Furthermore, many of the men and women—voters all—who are bombarding us with phone calls, see an added bonus in the Space Traders' offer." He looked around at his attentive cabinet members. "They are offering not only a solution to our nation's present problems but also one—surely an *ultimate* one—to what might be called the great American racial experiment. That's the real issue before us today. Does the promise of restored prosperity justify our sending away fifteen percent of our citizens to Lord knows what fate?"

"There are pluses and minuses to this 'fate' issue, Mr. President." Helen Hipmeyer, Secretary of Health and Human Services, usually remained silent at cabinet meetings. Her speaking up now caused eyebrows to rise around the table. "A large percentage of blacks rely on welfare and other social services. Their departure would ease substantially the burden on our state and national budgets. Why, the cost of caring for black AIDS victims alone has been extraordinary. On the other hand, the consternation and guilt among many whites if the blacks are sent away would take a severe psychological toll, with medical and other costs which might also reach astronomical levels. To gain the benefits we are discussing, without serious side effects, we must have more justification than I've heard thus far."

"Good point, Madame Secretary," the President answered, "but there are risks at every opportunity."

"I've never considered myself a particularly courageous individual, Mr. President." It was the Secretary of the Interior, a man small in stature but with a mind both sharp and devious, who had presided over the logging of the last of the old-growth timber in the nation's national forests. "But if I could guarantee prosperity for this great country by giving my life or going off with the Space Traders, I would do it without hesitation. And, if I would do it, I think every red-blooded American with an ounce of patriotism would as well." The Secretary sat down to the warm applause of his colleagues.

His suggestion kindled a thought in the Secretary of Defense. "Mr. President, the Secretary's courage is not unlike that American men and women have exhibited when called to military service. Some go more willingly than others, but almost all go even with the knowledge that they may not come back. It is a call a country makes on the assumption that its citizens will respond. I think that is the situation we have here, except that instead of just young men and women, the country needs all of its citizens of African descent to step forward and serve." More applause greeted this suggestion.

The Attorney General asked for and got the floor. "Mr. President, I think we could put together a legislative package modeled on the Selective Service Act of 1918. Courts have uniformly upheld this statute and its predecessors as being well within congressional power to exact enforced military duty at home or abroad by United States citizens.[2] While I don't see any constitutional problems, there would likely be quite a debate in Congress. But if the mail they are receiving is anything like ours, then the pressure for passage will be irresistible."

The President and the cabinet members heard reports from agents who had checked out samples of the gold, chemicals, and machinery the Space Traders had brought. More tests would be run in the next few days, but first indications

were that the gold was genuine, and that the antipollu-
tion chemicals and the nuclear fuel machine were safe and
worked. Everyone recognized that the benefits to the country
would be enormous. The ability to erase the country's debt
alone would ease the economic chaos the Federal Reserve
had staved off during the last few years only by its drastic—
the opposition party called it "unscrupulous"—manipulation of the money supply. The Secretary of the Treasury
confirmed that the Space Traders' gold would solve the nation's economic problems for decades to come.

"What are your thoughts on all this, Professor Golightly?"
asked the President, nodding at the scholarly-looking black
man sitting far down the table. The President realized that
there would be a lot more opposition to a selective service
plan among ordinary citizens than among the members of
his cabinet, and hoped Golightly would have some ideas for
getting around it.

Golightly began as though he understood the kind of answer the President wanted.

"As you know, Mr. President, I have supported this administration's policies that have led to the repeal of some
civil rights laws, to invalidation of most affirmative action
programs, and to severe reduction in appropriations for public assistance. To put it mildly, the positions of mine that have
received a great deal of media attention, have not been well
received in African-American communities. Even so, I have
been willing to be a 'good soldier' for the Party even though
I am condemned as an Uncle Tom by my people. I sincerely
believe that black people needed to stand up on their own

feet, free of special protection provided by civil rights laws, the suffocating burden of welfare checks, and the stigmatizing influence of affirmative action programs. In helping you undermine these policies, I realized that your reasons for doing so differed from mine. And yet I went along."

Golightly stopped. He reached down for his coffee mug, took a few sips, and ran his fingers through his graying but relatively straight (what some black people call "good") hair. "Mr. President, my record of support entitles me to be heard on the Space Traders' proposition. I disagree strongly with both the Secretary of the Interior and the Attorney General. What they are proposing is not universal selective service for blacks. It is group banishment, a most severe penalty and one that the Attorney General would impose without benefit of either due process or judicial review.

"It is a mark of just how far out of the mainstream black people are that this proposition is given any serious consideration. Were the Space Traders attracted by and asking to trade any other group—white women with red hair and green eyes, for example—a horrified public would order the visitors off the planet without a moment's hesitation. The revulsion would not be less because the number of persons with those physical characteristics are surely fewer than the twenty million black citizens you are ready to condemn to intergalactic exile.

"Mr. President, I cannot be objective on this proposal. I will match my patriotism, including readiness to give my life for my country, with that of the Secretary of the Interior. But my duty stops short of condemning my wife, my three children, my grandchildren, and my aged mother to an unknown fate. You simply cannot condemn twenty million people because they are black, and thus fit fodder for trade, so that this country can pay its debts, protect its environment, and ensure its energy supply. I am not ready to recommend such a sacrifice. Moreover, I doubt whether the Secretary of the Interior would willingly offer up his family and friends if the Space Traders sought them instead of me and mine." He paused.

"Professor Golightly," the Secretary of the Interior said, leaning forward, "the President asked you a specific question. This is not the time to debate which of us is the more patriotic or to engage in the details of the sacrifice that is a necessary component of any service for one's country."

Golightly chose to ignore the interruption. He knew, and the President knew, that his support—or, at least, his silent acquiescence—would be critical in winning undecided whites over to the selective service scheme. For their purposes, the President's media people had made Golightly an important voice on racial policy issues. They needed him now as never before.

"Mr. President," he continued, "you and your cabinet must place this offer in historical perspective. This is far from the first time this country's leaders have considered and rejected the removal of all those here of African descent. Benjamin Franklin and other abolitionists actively sought schemes to free the slaves and return them to their homeland. Lincoln examined and supported emigration programs both before and after he freed the slaves. Even those Radical Republicans who drafted the Civil War amendments wondered whether Africans could ever become a part of the national scene, a part of the American people.

"As early as 1866, Michigan's Senator Jacob Merritt Howard, an abolitionist and key architect of the Fourteenth Amendment, recognized the nation's need to confront the challenge posed by the presence of the former slaves, and spoke out on it, saying:

> For weal or for woe, the destiny of the colored race in this country is wrapped up with our own; they are to remain in our midst, and here spend their years and here bury their fathers and finally repose themselves. We may regret it. It may not be entirely compatible with our taste that they should live in our midst. We cannot help it. Our forefathers introduced them, and their destiny is to continue among us; and the practical question which now presents itself to us is as to the best mode of getting along with them.[3]

"Now, Mr. President, after receiving your invitation to this meeting, I had no difficulty in guessing its agenda or predicting how many of you might come down in favor of accepting the Space Traders' offer, and so looked up Senator Howard's speech. I have prepared copies of it for each of you. I recommend you study it."

Golightly walked around the large table to give each cabinet member a copy of the speech. As he did so, he pointed out, "The Senator's words are grudging rather than generous, conciliatory rather than crusading. He proposed sanctuary rather than equality for blacks. And though there have been periods in which their striving for full equality seems to have brought them close to their goal, sanctuary remains the more accurate description of black citizenship."

Returning to his place, Golightly continued. "This status has provided this nation an essential stability, one you sacrifice at your peril. With all due respect, Mr. President, acceptance of the Space Traders' solution will not bring a century of prosperity to this country. Secretary Hipmeyer is correct. What today seems to you a solution from Heaven will instead herald a decade of shame and dissension mirroring the moral conflicts that precipitated this nation into its most bloody conflict, the Civil War. The deep, self-inflicted wounds of that era have never really healed. Their reopening will inevitably lead to confrontations and strife that could cause the eventual dissolution of the nation."

"You seem to assume, Professor Golightly," the Secretary of the Interior interrupted again, "that the Space Traders want African Americans for some heinous purpose. Why do you ignore alternative scenarios? They are obviously aware of your people's plight here. Perhaps they have selected them to inhabit an interplanetary version of the biblical land of milk and honey. Or, more seriously," the Secretary said, "they may offer your people a new start in a less competitive environment, or"—he added, with a slight smirk in the President's direction—"perhaps they are going to give your people that training in skills and work discipline you're always urging on them."

No one actually laughed, but all except Golightly thought the Secretary's comment an excellent response to the black professor's gloomy predictions.

"I think we get your point, Professor," the President replied smoothly, concerned not to alienate a man whose support he would need. "We will give it weight in our considerations. Now," he said, rising, "we need to get to work on this thing. We don't have much time." He asked the Attorney General to draw up a rough draft of the proposed legislation by the end of the day, and told the rest of his cabinet that his aides would shortly be bringing them specific assignments. "Now let's all of us be sure to keep to ourselves what was said at this meeting"—and he glanced meaningfully at Professor Golightly. "Well, that's it for now, people. Meeting adjourned."

Long after the others had departed, Gleason Golightly sat at the long conference table. His hands were folded. He stared at the wall. He had always prided himself as the "man on the inside." While speaking in support of conservative policies, those were—he knew—policies that commanded enough support to be carried out. As a black man, his support legitimated those policies and salved the consciences of the whites who proposed and implemented them. A small price to pay, Golightly had always rationalized, for the many behind-the-scenes favors he received. The favors were not for himself. Golightly, a full professor at a small but well-endowed college, neither wanted nor needed what he called "blood money." Rather, he saw that black colleges got much-needed funding; and through his efforts, certain black officials received appointments or key promotions. He smiled wryly when some of these officials criticized his conservative positions and called him "Uncle Tom." He could bear that, knowing he made a contribution few others were able—or willing—to make to the racial cause.

Booker T. Washington was his hero and had been since he was a child growing up in a middle-class family in Alabama, not far from Tuskegee, the home of Tuskegee Institute, which Washington had founded in 1881. He had modeled his career on old Booker T., and while he did not have a following and had created no institutions, Golightly knew he had done more for black people than had a dozen of the loud-mouthed leaders who, he felt, talked much and produced little. But all of his life, he had dreamed of there coming a moment when his position as insider would enable him to perform some heroic act to both save his people great grief and gain for him the recognition and the love for which, despite his frequent denials, he knew he yearned.

Now, as he sat alone, he feared that this morning's meeting was that big chance, and he had failed it. The stakes, of course, were larger than he would have ever imagined they might be, and yet he thought he'd had the arguments. In retrospect, though, those arguments were based on morality and assumed a willingness on the part of the President and the cabinet to be fair, or at least to balance the benefits of the Trade against the sacrifice it would require of a selected portion of the American people. Instead of outsmarting them, Golightly had done what he so frequently criticized civil rights spokespersons for doing: he had tried to get whites to do right by black people because it was right that they do so. "Crazy!" he commented when civil rights people did it. "Crazy!" he mumbled to himself, at himself.

"Oh, Golightly, glad you're still here. I want a word with you." Golightly looked up as the Secretary of the Interior, at his most unctuous, eased himself into the seat beside him.

"Listen, old man, sorry about our differences at the meeting. I understand your concerns."

Golightly did not look at the man and, indeed, kept his eyes on the wall throughout their conversation. "What do you want, Mr. Secretary?"

The Secretary ignored Golightly's coldness. "You could tell in the meeting and from the media reports that this Trade thing is big, very big. There will be debate—as there should be in a great, free country like ours. But if I were a betting man, which I am not because of my religious beliefs, I would wager that this offer will be approved."

"I assume, Mr. Secretary, that to further the best interests of this *great, free* country of ours, you will be praying that the Trade is approved." Golightly's voice deepened ironically on the crucial words.

The Secretary's smile faded, and his eyes narrowed. "The President wants you to say whatever you can in favor of this plan."

"Why don't we simply follow your suggestion, Mr. Secretary, and tell everyone that the Space Traders are going to take the blacks to a land of milk and honey?"

The Secretary's voice hardened. "I don't think even black people are that stupid. No, Gleason, talk about patriotism, about the readiness of black people to make sacrifices for this country, about how they are really worthy citizens no matter what some may think. We'll leave the wording to you. Isn't sacrifice as proof of patriotism what your Frederick Douglass argued to get President Lincoln to open up the Union army to black enlistees?"

"And then?" Golightly asked, his eyes never moving from the wall.

"We know some blacks will escape. I understand some are leaving the country already. But"—and the Secretary's voice was smooth as butter—"if you go along with the program, Gleason, and the Trade is approved, the President says he'll see to it that one hundred black families are smuggled out of the country. You decide who they are. They'll include you and yours, of course."

Golightly said nothing.

After a moment of hesitation, the Secretary got up and strode to the door. Before leaving, he turned and said, "Think about it, Golightly. It's the kind of deal we think you should go for."

3 JANUARY. THE Anti-Trade Coalition—a gathering of black and liberal white politicians, civil rights representatives, and progressive academics—quickly assembled early that morning. Working nonstop and driven by anxiety to cooperate more than they ever had in the past, the members of the coalition had drafted a series of legal and political steps designed

to organize opposition to the Space Traders' offer. Constitutional challenges to any acceptance scheme were high on the list of opposition strategies. Bills opposing the Trade were drafted for early introduction in Congress. There were plans for direct action protests and boycotts. Finally, in the event that worse came to worst, and the administration decided to carry out what gathering participants were calling the "African-American kidnapping plot," a secret committee was selected to draft and distribute plans for massive disobedience.

Now, at close to midnight, the plenary session was ready to give final approval to this broad program of resistance.

At that moment, Professor Gleason Golightly sought the floor to propose an alternative response to the Trade offer. Golightly's close connection to the conservative administration and active support of its anti-black views made him far from a hero to most blacks. Many viewed his appearance at this critical hour as an administration-sponsored effort to undermine the coalition's defensive plans and tactics. At last, though, he prevailed on the conference leaders to grant him five minutes.

As he moved toward the podium, there was a wave of hostile murmuring whose justification Golightly acknowledged: "I am well aware that political and ideological differences have for several years sustained a wide chasm between us. But the events of two days ago have transformed our disputes into a painful reminder of our shared status. I am here because, whatever our ideological differences or our socioeconomic positions, we all know that black rights, black interests, black property, even black lives are expendable whenever their sacrifice will further or sustain white needs or preferences."

Hearing Golightly admitting to truths he had long denied served to silence the murmuring. "It has become an unwritten tradition in this country for whites to sacrifice our rights to further their own interests. This tradition overshadows the national debate about the Space Traders' offer and may well foretell our reply to it."

Oblivious of the whites in the audience, Golightly said, "I realize that our liberal white friends continue to reassure us. 'This is America,' they tell us. 'It can't happen here.' But I've noticed that those whites who are most vigorous in their assurances are least able to rebut the contrary teaching of both historic fact and present reality. Outside civil rights gatherings like this, the masses of black people—those you claim to represent but to whom you seldom listen—are mostly resigned to the nation's acceptance of the Space Traders' offer. For them, liberal optimism is smothered by their life experience.

"Black people know for a fact what you, their leaders, fear to face. Black people know your plans for legislation, litigation, and protest cannot prevail against the tradition of sacrificing black rights. Indeed, your efforts will simply add a veneer of face-saving uncertainty to a debate whose outcome is not only predictable, but inevitable. Flying in the face of our history, you are still relying on the assumption that whites really want to grant justice to blacks, really want to alleviate onerous racial conditions."

"Professor Golightly," the chairman interrupted, "the time we have allotted you has almost expired. The delegates here are weary and anxious to return to their homes so that they can assist their families through this crisis. The defense plans we have formulated are our best effort. Sir, if you have a better way, let us hear it now."

Golightly nodded. "I promised to be brief, and I will. Although you have labored here unselfishly to devise a defense against what is surely the most dangerous threat to our survival since our forebears were kidnapped from Africa's shores. I think I have a better way, and I urge you to hear it objectively and without regard to our past differences. The question is how best to counter an offer that about a third of the voters would support even if the Space Traders offered America nothing at all. Another third may vacillate, but we both know that in the end they will simply not be able to pass up a good deal. The only way we can deflect, and perhaps reverse, a process that is virtually certain to result in approval of the Space Traders' offer, is to give up the oppositional stance you are about to adopt, and forthrightly urge the country to accept the Space Traders' offer."

He paused, looking out over the sea of faces. Then there was a clamor of outraged cries: "Sell-out!" "Traitor!" and "Ultimate Uncle Tom!" The chairman banged his gavel in an effort to restore order.

Seemingly unmoved by the outburst, Golightly waited until the audience quieted, then continued. "A major, perhaps the principal, motivation for racism in this country is the deeply held belief that black people should not have anything that white people don't have. Not only do whites insist on better jobs, higher incomes, better schools and neighborhoods, better everything, but they also usurp aspects of our culture. They have 'taken our blues and gone,' to quote Langston Hughes[4]—songs that sprang from our very subordination. Whites exploit not only our music but our dance, language patterns, dress, and hair styles as well. Even the badge of our inferior status, our color, is not sacrosanct, whites spending billions a year to emulate our skin tones, paradoxically, as a sign of their higher status. So whites' appropriation of what is ours and their general acquisitiveness are facts—facts we must make work for us. Rather than resisting the Space Traders' offer, let us circulate widely the rumor that the Space Traders, aware of our long fruitless struggle on this planet, are arranging to transport us to a land of milk and honey—a virtual paradise.

"Remember, most whites are so jealous of their race-based prerogatives that they oppose affirmative action even though many of these programs would remove barriers that exclude whites as well as blacks. Can we not expect such whites—notwithstanding even the impressive benefits offered by the Space Traders—to go all out to prevent blacks from gaining access to an extraterrestrial New Jerusalem? Although you are planning to litigate against the Trade on the grounds that it is illegal discrimination to limit it to black people, mark my words, our 'milk and honey' story will inspire whites to institute such litigation on the grounds that limiting the Space Traders' offer to black people is unconstitutional discrimination against whites!

"Many of you have charged that I have become expert at manipulating white people for personal gain. Although profit has not in fact motivated my actions, I certainly have learned to understand how whites think on racial issues. On that knowledge, I am willing to wage my survival and that of my family. I urge you to do the same. This strategy is, however, risky, our only hope."

The murmurs had subsided into stony silence by the time Golightly left the podium.

"Does anyone care to respond to Professor Golightly's suggestion?" the chairman finally asked.

Justin Jasper, a well-known and highly respected Baptist minister, came to the microphone. "I readily concede Dr. Golightly's expertise in the psychology of whites' thinking. Furthermore, as he requests, I hold in abeyance my deep distrust of a black man whose willing service to whites has led him to become a master minstrel of political mimicry. But my problem with his plan is twofold. First, it rings hollow because it so resembles Dr. Golightly's consistent opposition in the past to all our civil rights initiatives. Once again, he is urging us to accept rather than oppose a racist policy. And, not only are we not to resist, but we are to beg the country to lead us to the sacrificial altar. God may have that power, but Dr. Golightly is not my god!"

The Reverend Jasper was a master orator, and he quickly had his audience with him. "Second, because the proposal lacks truth, it insults my soul. In the forty years I have worked for civil rights, I have lost more battles than I have won, but I have never lost my integrity. Telling the truth about racism has put me in prison and many of my co-workers into early graves.

"The truth is, Dr. Golightly, that what this country is ready to do to us is wrong! It is evil! It is an action so heinous as to give the word *betrayal* a bad name. I can speak only for myself, but even if I were certain that my family and I could escape the threat we now face by lying about our likely fate—and, Dr. Golightly, that is what you're asking us to do—I do not choose to save myself by a tactic that may preserve my body at the sacrifice of my soul. The fact is, Dr. Golightly, until my Lord calls me home, I do not want to leave this country even for a land of milk and honey. My people were brought here involuntarily, and that is the only way they're going to get me out!"

The Reverend Jasper received a standing ovation. Many people were crying openly as they applauded. After thanking them, the minister asked everyone to join in singing the old nineteenth-century hymn "Amazing Grace," which, he reminded them, had been written by an English minister, one John Newton, who as a young man and before finding God's grace, had been captain of a slave ship. It was with special fervor that they sang the verse:

> *Through many dangers, toils, and snares,*
> *I have already come.*
> *'Twas grace that brought me safe this far,*
> *And grace will lead me home.*[5]

With the hymn's melody still resonating, the coalition's members voted unanimously to approve their defensive package. The meeting was quickly adjourned. Leaving the hall, everyone agreed that they had done all that could be done to oppose approval of the Space Traders' offer. As for Golightly, his proposal was dismissed as coming from a person who, in their view, had so often sold out black interests. "He's a sad case. Even with this crisis, he's just doing what he's always done."

Again, as after the President's cabinet meeting, Golightly sat for a long time alone. He did not really mind that none of the delegates had spoken to him before leaving. But he was crushed by his failure to get them to recognize what he had long known: that without power, a people must use cunning and guile. Or were cunning and guile, based on superior understanding of a situation, themselves power? Certainly, most black people knew and used this art to survive in their everyday contacts with white people. It was only civil rights professionals who confused integrity with foolhardiness.

"Faith in God is fine," Golightly muttered to himself. "But God expects us to use the common sense He gave us to get out of life-threatening situations."

Still, castigation of black leadership could not alter the fact. Golightly had failed, and he knew it. Sure, he was smarter than they were—smarter even than most whites; but he had finally outsmarted himself. At the crucial moment, when he most needed to help his people, both whites and blacks had rejected as untrustworthy both himself and his plans.

4 JANUARY. IN a nationally televised address, the President sought to reassure both Trade supporters that he was

responding favorably to their strong messages, and blacks and whites opposed to the Trade that he would not ignore their views. After the usual patriotic verbiage, the President said that just-completed, end-of-century economic reports revealed the nation to be in much worse shape than anyone had imagined. He summarized what he called the "very grim figures," and added that only massive new resources would save America from having to declare bankruptcy.

"On the face of it, our visitors from outer space have initiated their relationship with our country in a most unusual way. They are a foreign power and as such entitled to the respect this nation has always granted to the family of nations on Earth; it is not appropriate for us to prejudge this extra-planetary nation's offer. Thus, it is now receiving careful study and review by this administration.

"Of course, I am aware of the sacrifice that some of our most highly regarded citizens would be asked to make in the proposed trade. While these citizens are of only one racial group, there is absolutely no evidence whatsoever to indicate that the selection was intended to discriminate against any race or religion or ethnic background.

"No decisions have been made, and all options are under review. This much seems clear: the materials the Traders have offered us are genuine and perform as promised. Early estimates indicate that, if these materials were made available to this nation, they would solve our economic crisis, and we could look forward to a century of unparalleled prosperity. Whether the Trade would allow a tax-free year for every American, as some of our citizens have hoped, is not certain.

But I can promise that if the Trade is approved, I will exercise my best efforts to make such a trade dividend a reality."

Early that morning, the leaders of Fortune-500 businesses, heads of banks, insurance companies, and similar entities boarded their well-appointed corporate jets and flew to a remote Wyoming hunting lodge. They understood the President supported the Trade, despite his avowals that no decision had been made. They had come to discuss the Trade offer's implications for big business.

5 JANUARY. NOT content with just closing the doors on their meeting as the Anti-Trade Coalition had, the corporate leaders of America gathered for an absolutely hush-hush meeting. They were joined by the Vice President and some of the wealthier members of Congress. The surroundings were beautiful, but the gathering of white males was somber. Corporate America faced a dilemma of its own making.

Media polls as well as ones privately funded by businesses all reported tremendous public support for the Trade— unhappy but hardly unexpected news for the nation's richest and most powerful men. First, blacks represented 12 percent of the market and generally consumed much more of their income than did their white counterparts. No one wanted to send that portion of the market into outer space—not even for the social and practical benefits offered by the Space Traders.

Even those benefits were a mixed blessing. Coal and oil companies, expecting to raise their prices as supplies steadily decreased, were not elated at the prospect of an inexhaustible energy source; it could quickly put them out of business. Similarly, businesses whose profits were based on sales in black ghetto communities—or who supplied law enforcement agencies, prisons, and other such institutions—faced substantial losses in sales. The real estate industry, for example, annually reaped uncounted millions in commissions on sales and rentals, inflated by the understanding that blacks would not be allowed to purchase or rent in an area. Even these concerns were overshadowed by fears of what the huge influx of gold to pay all state debts would do to the economy or to the value of either the current money supply or gold.

Though seldom acknowledging the fact, most business leaders understood that blacks were crucial in stabilizing the economy with its ever-increasing disparity between the incomes of rich and poor. They recognized that potentially turbulent unrest among those on the bottom was deflected by the continuing efforts of poorer whites to ensure that they, at least, remained ahead of blacks. If blacks were removed from the society, working- and middle-class whites— deprived of their racial distraction—might look upward toward the top of the societal well and realize that they as well as the blacks below them suffered because of the gross disparities in opportunities and income.

Many of these corporate leaders and their elected representatives had for years exploited poor whites' ignorance of their real enemy. Now, what had been a comforting insulation of their privileges and wealth posed a serious barrier to what a majority saw as a first priority: to persuade the country to reject the Trade. A quick survey of the media and advertising representatives present was not encouraging. "It would be quite a challenge," one network executive said, "but we simply can't change this country's view about the superiority of whites and the inferiority of blacks in a week. I doubt you could do it in a decade."

Even so, the corporate leaders decided to try. They planned to launch immediately a major media campaign— television, radio, and the press—to exploit both the integration achieved in America and the moral cost of its loss. White members of professional and college sports teams would urge rejection of the Trade "so as to keep the team together." Whites in integrated businesses, schools, churches, and neighborhoods would broadcast similar messages. The business leaders even committed large sums to facilitate campaigning by pro-choice womens' groups who were strongly anti-Trade. In a particularly poignant series of ads, white spouses in interracial marriages would point out that the Trade would destroy their families, and beg the public not to support it.

Newspaper and magazine publishers promised supportive editorials, but the Vice President and other government representatives argued that the immediate political gains from accepting the Trade would translate into business benefits as well.

"With all due respect, Mr. Vice President," he was told, "that argument shows why you are in politics and we are in business. It also shows that you are not listening very closely to those of us whose campaign contributions put you in office."

"We need your financial support," the Vice President admitted, "but our polls show most white voters favor the Trade, and the administration is under increasing pressure to do the same. And, as you know, pro-Trade advocates are promising that with all government debts paid, every American would get a year without any taxes. Believe it or not, some liberal environmentalists are thinking of giving their support to the Trade as the lesser of two evils. Of course, the prospect of heating and air-conditioning homes without paying through the nose is very appealing, even to those who don't care a hoot about the environment."

"However enticing such benefits of the Trade may be," interjected a government census official, "the real attraction for a great many whites is that it would remove black people from this society. Since the first of the year, my staff and I have interviewed literally thousands of citizens across the country, and, though they don't say it directly, it's clear that at bottom they simply think this will be a better country without black people. I fear, gentlemen, that those of us who have been perpetuating this belief over the years have done a better job than we knew."

"I must add what you probably already know," the Vice President broke in, "that the administration is leaning toward acceptance of the Space Traders' offer. Now, if you fellows line up against the Trade, it could make a difference—but, in that case, the President may opt to build on the phony populist image you provided him in his first election campaign. He knows that the working- and middle-class white people in this country want the blacks to go, and if they get a chance to express their real views in the privacy of a polling place, the Trade plan will pass overwhelmingly."

"Bullshit!" roared a billionaire who had made his fortune in construction. "I'm sick of this defeatist talk! We need to get off our dead asses and get to work on this thing. Everyone says that money talks. Well dammit, let's get out there and spend some money. If this thing goes to a public referendum, we can buy whatever and whoever is necessary. It sure as hell will not be the first time," he wound up, pounding both fists on the long conference table, "and likely not the last!"

The remainder of the meeting was more upbeat. Pointedly telling the Vice President that he and the administration were caught in the middle and would have to decide whose support they most wanted in the future, the business leaders began making specific plans to suspend all regular broadcasting and, through 16 January, to air nothing but anti-Trade ads and special Trade programs. They flew out that night, their confidence restored. They controlled the media. They had become rich and successful "playing hard ball." However competitive with one another, they had, as usual, united to confront this new challenge to their hegemony. It was, as usual, inconceivable that they could fail.

6 JANUARY. ALTHOUGH the Television Evangelists of America also owned jets, they understood that their power lay less in these perks of the wealthy than in their own ability to manipulate their TV congregations' religious feelings. So, after a lengthy conference call, they announced a massive evangelical rally in the Houston Astrodome which would be televised over their religious cable network. They went all out. The Trade offer was the evangelists' chance to rebuild their prestige and fortunes, neither of which had recovered from the Jim and Tammy Bakker and the Jimmy Swaggart scandals. They would achieve this much-desired goal by playing on, rather than trying to change, the strongly racist views of their mostly working-class television audiences. True, some of the preachers had a substantial black following, but evangelical support for the Trade would not be the evangelists' decision. Rather, these media messiahs heralded it as God's will.

The Space Traders were, according to the televised "Gospel," bringing America blessings earned by their listeners' and viewers' faithful dedication to freedom, liberty, and God's word. Not only would rejection of these blessings from space be wrong, so the preachers exhorted; it would be blasphemous. It was God's will that all Americans enjoy a tax-free year, a cleaned-up environment for years to come, and cheap heating forever. True, a sacrifice was required if they were to obtain God's bounty—a painful sacrifice. But here, too, God was testing Americans, his chosen people, to ensure that they were worthy of His bounty, deserving of His love. Each preacher drew on Scripture, tortuously interpreted, to support these statements.

A "ministry of music" quartet—four of the most popular television evangelists, all speaking in careful cadences like a white rap group—preached the major sermon. It whipped the crowd into a delirium of religious feeling, making them receptive both to the financial appeals, which raised millions, and to the rally's grande finale: a somber tableau of black people marching stoically into the Space Traders' ships, which here resembled ancient sacrificial altars. Try as they might, the producers of the pageant had had a hard time finding black people willing to act out roles they might soon be forced to experience, but a few blacks were glad to be paid handsomely for walking silently across the stage. These few were easily supplemented by the many whites eager to daub on "black face."

The rally was a great success despite the all-out efforts of the media to condemn this "sacrilege of all that is truly holy." That night, millions of messages, all urging acceptance of the Space Traders' offer, deluged the President and Congress.

7 JANUARY. GROUPS supporting the Space Traders' proposition had from the beginning taken seriously blacks' charges that acceptance of it would violate the Constitution's most basic protections. Acting swiftly, and with the full cooperation of the states, they had set in motion the steps necessary to convene a constitutional convention in Philadelphia. ("Of course!" groaned Golightly when he heard of it.) And there, on this day, on the site of the original constitutional convention, delegates—chosen, in accordance with Article V of the Constitution, by the state legislatures—quickly drafted, and by a substantial majority passed, the Twenty-seventh Amendment to the Constitution of the United States. It declared:

Without regard to the language or interpretations previously given any other provision of this document, every United States citizen is subject at the call of Congress to selection for special service for periods necessary to protect domestic interests and international needs.

The amendment was scheduled for ratification by the states on 15 January in a national referendum. If ratified, the amendment would validate amendments to existing selective service laws authorizing the induction of all blacks into special service for transportation under the terms of the Space Traders' offer.

8 JANUARY. LED by Rabbi Abraham Specter, a group of Jewish church and organizational leaders sponsored a mammoth anti-Trade rally in New York's Madison Square Garden. "We simply cannot stand by and allow America's version of the Final Solution to its race problem to be carried out without our strong protest and committed opposition." Thirty-five thousand Jews signed pledges to disrupt by all possible nonviolent means both the referendum and—if the amendment was ratified—the selection of blacks for 'special service.'

"Already," Rabbi Specter announced, "a secret Anne Frank Committee has formed, and its hundreds of members have begun to locate hiding places in out-of-the-way sites across this great country. Blacks by the thousands can be hidden for years if necessary until the nation returns to its senses.

"We vow this action because we recognize the fateful parallel between the plight of the blacks in this country and the situation of the Jews in Nazi Germany. Holocaust scholars agree that the Final Solution in Germany would not have been possible without the pervasive presence and the uninterrupted tradition of anti-Semitism in Germany. We must not let the Space Traders be the final solution for blacks in America."

A concern of many Jews not contained in their official condemnations of the Trade offer was that, in the absence of blacks, Jews could become the scapegoats for a system so reliant on an identifiable group on whose heads less-well-off whites can discharge their hate and frustrations for societal disabilities about which they are unwilling to confront their leaders. Given the German experience, few Jews argued that "it couldn't happen here."[6]

9 JANUARY. RESPONDING almost immediately to the Jewish anti-Trade rally, the Attorney General expressed his "grave concern" that what he felt certain was but a small group of Jews would, by acting in flagrant violation of the law of the land, besmirch the good names of all patriotic American Jews. For this reason, he said, he was releasing for publication the secret list, obtained by undercover FBI agents, of all those who had joined the Anne Frank Committee. He stated that the release was needed so that all Americans could easily distinguish this group from the majority of patriotic and law-abiding Jewish citizens.

Retaliation was quick. Within hours, men and women listed as belonging to the committee lost their jobs; their contracts were canceled; their mortgages foreclosed; and harassment of them, including physical violence, escalated into a nationwide resurgence of anti-Semitic feeling. Groups on the far right, who were exploiting the growing support for the Trade, urged: "Send the blacks into space. Send the Jews into Hell." The Jews who opposed the Trade were intimidated into silence and inaction. The leaders of Rabbi Specter's group were themselves forced into hiding, leaving few able to provide any haven for blacks.

10 JANUARY. IN the brief but intense pre–election day campaign, the pro-ratification groups' major argument had an appeal that surprised even those who made it. Their message was straightforward:

The Framers intended America to be a white country. The evidence of their intentions is present in the original Constitution. After more than a hundred and thirty-seven years of good-faith efforts to build a healthy, stable interracial nation, we have concluded—as the Framers did in the beginning—that our survival today requires that we sacrifice the rights of blacks in order to protect and further the interests of whites. The Framers' example must be our guide. Patriotism, and not pity, must govern our decision. We should ratify the amendment and accept the Space Traders' proposition.

In response, a coalition of liberal opponents to the Space Traders' offer sought to combine pragmatism and principle in what they called their "slippery Trade slope" argument. First, they proclaimed the strong moral position that trading away a group of Americans identifiable by race is wrong and violates our basic principles. The coalition aimed its major thrust, however, at the self-interest of white Americans: "Does not consigning blacks to an unknown fate set a dangerous precedent?" the liberals demanded. "Who will be next?"

In full-page ads, they pressed the point: "Are we cannibals ready to consume our own for profit? And if we are, the blacks may be only the first. If the Space Traders return with an irresistible offer for another group, the precedent will have been set, and none of us will be safe. Certainly not the minorities—Hispanics, Jews, Asians—and perhaps not even those of us identifiable by politics or religion or geographic location. Setting such a precedent of profit could consume us all."

Astutely sidestepping the Trade precedent arguments, the pro-Trade response focused on the past sacrifices of blacks. "In each instance," it went, "the sacrifice of black rights was absolutely necessary to accomplish an important government purpose. These decisions were neither arbitrary nor capricious. Without the compromises on slavery in the Constitution of 1787, there would be no America. Nor would there be any framework under which those opposed to slavery could continue the struggle that eventually led to the Civil War and emancipation.

"And where and how might slavery have ended had a new government not been formed? On what foundation would the post–Civil War amendments been appended? Sacrifices by blacks were made, but those sacrifices were both necessary and eventually rewarding to blacks as well as the nation."

In countering the anti-Trade contention that the sacrifice of black rights was both evil and unprecedented, pro-Traders claimed, "Beginning with the Civil War in which black people gained their liberty, this nation has called on its people to serve in its defense. Many men and women have voluntarily enlisted in the armed services, but literally millions of men have been conscripted, required to serve their country, and, if necessary, to sacrifice not simply their rights but also their lives."

As for the argument that the sacrifice of black rights in political compromises was odious racial discrimination, pro-Trade forces contended that "fortuitous fate and not blatant racism" should be held responsible. Just as men and not women are inducted into the military, and even then only men of a certain age and physical and mental condition, so only some groups are destined by their role in the nation's history to serve as catalyst for stability and progress.

"All Americans are expected to make sacrifices for the good of their country. Black people are no exceptions to this basic obligation of citizenship. Their role may be special, but so is that of many of those who serve. The role that blacks may be called on to play in response to the Space Traders' offer is, however regrettable, neither immoral nor unconstitutional."

A tremendous groundswell of public agreement with the pro-Trade position drowned out anti-Trade complaints of unfairness. Powerful as would have been the notion of seeing the Space Traders' offer as no more than a fortuitous circumstance, in which blacks might be called on to sacrifice for their country, the "racial sacrifice as historic necessity" argument made the pro-Trade position irresistible to millions of voters—and to their Congressional representatives.

11 January. Unconfirmed media reports asserted that U.S. officials tried in secret negotiations to get the Space Traders to take in trade only those blacks currently under the jurisdiction of the criminal justice system—that is, in prison or on parole or probation. Government negotiators noted that this would include almost one half of the black males in the twenty- to twenty-nine-year-old age bracket.* Negotiators were also reported to have offered to trade only blacks locked in the inner cities. But the Space Traders stated that they had no intention of turning their far-off homeland into an American prison colony for blacks. In rejecting the American offer, the Space Traders warned that they would withdraw their proposition unless the United States halted the flight of the growing numbers of middle-class blacks who— fearing the worst—were fleeing the country.

---

* In 1990, the figure was 24 percent, according to Justice Department data contained in a study funded by the Rand Corporation.[7] The National Center on Institutions and Alternatives reported that 42 percent of the black men in the District of Columbia, aged eighteen through thirty-five, were enmeshed in the criminal justice system on any given day in 1991.[8]

In response, executive orders were issued and implemented, barring blacks from leaving the country until the Space Traders' proposition was fully debated and resolved. "It is your patriotic duty," blacks were told by the White House, "to allow this great issue to be resolved through the democratic process and in accordance with the rule of law." To ensure that the Trade debate and referendum were concluded in a "noncoercive environment," all blacks serving in the military were placed on furlough and relieved of their weapons. State officials took similar action with respect to blacks on active duty in state and local police forces.

12 JANUARY. THE Supreme Court, citing precedent dating back to 1849, rejected a number of appeals by blacks and their white supporters whose legal challenges to every aspect of the referendum process had been dismissed by lower courts as "political questions" best resolved by the body politic rather than through judicial review.[9]

The Supreme Court's order refusing to intervene in the Space Trader proposition was unanimous. The order was brief and *per curiam,* the Court agreeing that the Space Trader litigation lacked judicially discoverable and manageable standards for resolving the issues.[10] The Court also noted that, if inducted in accordance with a constitutionally approved conscription provision, blacks would have no issues of individual rights for review. Even if the Court were to conclude that rights under the Fourteenth Amendment were deserving of greater weight than the authority of the new constitutional amendment up for ratification, the standards of national necessity that prompted the Court to approve the confinement of Japanese Americans during the Second World War[11] would serve as sufficient precedent for the induction and transfer of African Americans to the Space Traders.

While not claiming to give weight to the public opinion polls reporting strong support for the Trade, the Court noted that almost a century earlier, in 1903, Justice Oliver Wendell Holmes had denied injunctive relief to six thousand blacks who petitioned the Court to protect their right to vote.[12] The bill alleged that the great mass of the white population intended to keep the blacks from voting; but, in view of such massive opposition, Holmes reasoned that ordering the blacks' names to be placed on the voting list would be "an empty form" unless the Court also mandated electoral supervision by "officers of the court."[*]

14 JANUARY. WITH the legal questions of the Trade resolved, the U.S. government announced that as a result of intensive negotiations with the Space Trader leaders, the latter had agreed to amend their offer and exclude from the Trade all black people seventy years old, and older, and all those blacks who were seriously handicapped, ill, and injured. In addition, a thousand otherwise-eligible blacks and their

---

[*] Justice Holmes wrote: "Unless we are prepared to supervise the voting in that state by officers of the court, it seems to us that all the plaintiff could get from equity would be an empty form. Apart from damages to the individual, relief from a great political wrong, if done, as alleged, by the people of a state and the state itself, must be given by them or by the legislature and political department of the Government of the United States."[13]

immediate families would be left behind as trustees of black property and possessions, all of which were to be stored or held in escrow in case blacks were returned to this country. Each of the thousand black "detainees" was required to pledge to accept a subordinate status with "suspended citizenship" until such time as the "special service inductees" were returned to the country. The administration selected blacks to remain who had records of loyalty to the conservative party and no recorded instances of militant activity. Even so, many of those blacks selected declined to remain. "We will, like the others," said one black who rejected detainee status, "take our chances with the referendum."

15 JANUARY. MANY whites had, to their credit, been working day and night to defeat the amendment; but, as is the usual fate of minority rights when subjected to referenda or initiatives,[14] the outcome was never really in doubt. The final vote tally confirmed the predictions. By 70 percent to 30 percent, American citizens voted to ratify the constitutional amendment that provided a legal basis for acceptance of the Space Traders' offer. In anticipation of this result, government agencies had secretly made preparations to facilitate the transfer. Some blacks escaped, and many thousands lost their lives in futile efforts to resist the joint federal and state police teams responsible for rounding up, cataloguing, and transporting blacks to the coast.

16 JANUARY. PROFESSOR Golightly and his family were not granted detainee status. Instead, the White House promised

him safe passage to Canada for all his past services even though he had not made the patriotic appeal the President had requested of him. But, at the border that evening, he was stopped and turned back. It turned out the Secretary of the Interior had called to countermand his departure. Golightly was not surprised. What really distressed him was his failure to convince the black leaders of the anti-Trade coalition to heed their own rhetoric: namely that whites in power would, given the chance, do to privileged blacks what, in fact, they had done to all blacks.

"I wonder," he murmured, half to himself, half to his wife, as they rode in a luxury limousine sent, in some irony, by the Secretary of the Interior to convey them to the nearest roundup point, "how my high-minded brothers at the conference feel now about their decision to fail with integrity rather than stoop to the bit of trickery that might have saved them."

"But, Gleason," his wife asked, "would our lives have really been better had we fooled the country into voting against the Trade? If the Space Traders were to depart, carrying away with them what they and everyone else says can solve our major domestic problems, wouldn't people increasingly blame us blacks for increases in debt, pollution, and fuel shortages? We might have saved ourselves—but only to face here a fate as dire as any we face in space."

"I hope your stoic outlook helps us through whatever lies ahead," Golightly responded as the car stopped. Then guards hustled him and his family toward the buses being loaded with other blacks captured at the Canadian border.

17 JANUARY. THE last Martin Luther King holiday the nation would ever observe dawned on an extraordinary sight. In the night, the Space Traders had drawn their strange ships right up to the beaches and discharged their cargoes of gold, minerals, and machinery, leaving vast empty holds. Crowded on the beaches were the inductees, some twenty million silent black men, women, and children, including babes in arms. As the sun rose, the Space Traders directed them, first, to strip off all but a single undergarment; then, to line up; and finally, to enter those holds which yawned in the morning light like Milton's "darkness visible." The inductees looked fearfully behind them. But, on the dunes above the beaches, guns at the ready, stood U.S. guards. There was no escape, no alternative. Heads bowed, arms now linked by slender chains, black people left the New World as their forebears had arrived.

Beyond Despair

DEAR GENEVA,

Beyond the despair of your final narrative, I am reminded that our forebears—though betrayed into bondage—survived the slavery in which they were reduced to things, property, entitled neither to rights nor to respect as human beings. Somehow, as the legacy of our spirituals makes clear, our enslaved ancestors managed to retain their humanity as well as their faith that evil and suffering were not the extent of their destiny—or of the destiny of those who would follow them. Indeed, we owe our existence to their perseverance, their faith. In these perilous times, we must do no less than they did: fashion a philosophy that both matches the unique dangers we face, and enables us to recognize in those dangers opportunities for committed living and humane service.

The task is less daunting than it might appear. From the beginning, we have been living and working for racial justice in the face of unacknowledged threat. Thus, we are closer than we may realize to those in slavery who struggled to begin and maintain families even though at any moment they might be sold, and separated, never to see one another again. Those blacks living in the pre–Civil War North, though deemed "free," had to live with the ever-present knowledge that the underground railroad ran both ways. While abolitionists provided an illegal network to aid blacks who escaped slavery, Southern "slave catchers" had an equally extensive system that enabled them to kidnap free blacks from their homes or the streets, and spirit them off to the South and a life in bondage.[1]

In those times, racism presented dangers from without that were stark and terrifying, but they were hardly more insidious than those blacks face today in our inner cities—all too often from other blacks. Victimized themselves by an uncaring society, some young blacks vent their rage on victims like themselves, thereby perpetuating the terror that whites once had to invoke directly. We should not be surprised that a society that once legalized slavery and authorized pursuit of fugitive slaves with little concern about the kidnapping of free blacks, now views black-on-black crime as basically a problem for its victims and their communities.

In the context of such a history, played out now as current events, is a long continuum of risks faced and survived, our oppression barring our oppressors from actually experiencing the freedom they so proudly proclaim. The late Harvard historian Nathan Huggins points out in *Black Odyssey*, a book about slavery from the point of view of the slaves:

"Uncertainty, the act of being engaged in an unknown and evolving future, was their common fate. In the indefinite was the excitement of the possible. . . . That sense of possibility and that dream have infected all Americans, Africans no less than Europeans. . . . *Yet the dream has been elusive to us all,* white and black, from that first landfall [at Jamestown where the first twenty Africans landed]."[2]

Huggins argues that Americans view history as linear and evolutionary and tend to see slavery and racism as an aberration or pathological condition: "Our national history has continued to amplify the myths of automatic progress, universal freedom, and the American dream without the ugly reality of racism seriously challenging the faith."[3] Those who accept these myths, consider our view that racism is permanent to be despairing, defeatist, and wrong. In so doing, they overlook the fact that the "American dogma of automatic progress fails those who have been marginalized. Blacks, the poor, and others whom the myth ignores are conspicuously in the center of the present, and they call for a national history that incorporates their experience."[4]

Such a new narrative, and the people who make it—among whom are included those who pursue equality through legal means—must find inspiration not in the sacrosanct, but utterly defunct, glory of ideals that for centuries have proven both unattainable and poisonous. Rather, they must find it in the lives of our "oppressed people who defied social death as slaves and freedmen, insisting on their humanity despite a social consensus that they were 'a brutish sort of people.'"[5]

From that reality, Huggins takes—as do you and I, Geneva—
hope rather than despair. Knowing there was no escape, no
way out, the slaves, nonetheless continued to engage themselves. To carve out a humanity. To defy the murder of self-
hood. Their lives were brutally shackled, certainly—but *not
without meaning despite being imprisoned.*[6]

We are proud of our heroes, but we must not forget those
whose lives were not marked by extraordinary acts of defiance. Though they lived and died as captives within a system
of slave labor, "they produced worlds of music, poetry, and
art. They reshaped a Christian cosmology to fit their spirits and their needs, transforming Protestantism along the
way. They produced a single people out of what had been
many.... Their ordeal, and their dignity throughout it,
speaks to the world of the indomitable human spirit."[7]

Perhaps those of us who can admit we are imprisoned by
the history of racial subordination in America can accept—
as slaves had no choice but to accept—our fate. Not that we
legitimate the racism of the oppressor. On the contrary, we
can only *de*legitimate it if we can accurately pinpoint it. And
racism lies at the center, not the periphery; in the permanent,
not in the fleeting; in the real lives of black and white people,
not in the sentimental caverns of the mind.

Armed with this knowledge, and with the enlightened,
humility-based commitment that it engenders, we can accept
the dilemmas of committed confrontation with evils we cannot end. We can go forth to serve, knowing that our failure
to act will not change conditions and may very well worsen

them. We can listen carefully to those who have been most subordinated. In listening, we must not do them the injustice of failing to recognize that somehow they survived as complete, defiant, though horribly scarred beings. We must learn from their example, learn from those whom we would teach.

If we are to extract solutions from the lessons of the slaves' survival, and our own, we must first face squarely the unbearable landscape and climate of that survival. We yearn that our civil rights work will be crowned with success, but what we really want—want even more than success—is meaning. "Meaningfulness," as the Stanford psychiatrist Dr. Irvin Yalom tells us, "is a by-product of engagement and commitment."[8] This engagement and commitment is what black people have had to do since slavery: making something out of nothing. Carving out a humanity for oneself with absolutely nothing to help—save imagination, will, and unbelievable strength and courage. Beating the odds while firmly believing in, *knowing* as only they could know, the fact that all those odds are stacked against them.

Both engagement and commitment connote service. And genuine service requires humility. We must first recognize and acknowledge (at least to ourselves) that our actions are not likely to lead to transcendent change and may indeed, despite our best efforts, be of more help to the system we despise than to the victims of that system whom we are trying to help. Then, and only then, can that realization and the dedication based on it lead to policy positions and campaigns that are less likely to worsen conditions for those we are trying to help and more likely to remind the powers that be that out there are persons like us who are not only not on their side but determined to stand in their way.

Now there is more here than confrontation with our oppressors. Continued struggle can bring about unexpected benefits and gains that in themselves justify continued endeavor. We can recognize miracles we did not plan and value them for what they are, rather than always measure their worth by their likely contribution to our traditional goals. As a former student, Erin Edmonds, concludes, it is not a matter of choosing between the pragmatic recognition that racism is permanent no matter what we do, or an idealism based on the long-held dream of attaining a society free of racism. Rather, it is a question of *both, and*. *Both* the recognition of the futility of action—where action is more civil rights strategies destined to fail—*and* the unalterable conviction that something must be done, that action must be taken.[9]

This is, I believe, a more realistic perspective from which to gauge the present and future worth of our race-related activities. Freed of the stifling rigidity of relying unthinkingly on the slogan "we shall overcome," we are impelled *both* to live each day more fully *and* to examine critically the actual effectiveness of traditional civil rights remedies. Indeed, the humility required by genuine service will not permit us to urge remedies that we may think appropriate and the law may even require, but that the victims of discrimination have rejected.

That, Geneva, is the real Black History, all too easily lost in political debates over curricular needs. It is a story less of success than of survival through an unremitting struggle that leaves no room for giving up. We are all part of that history, and it is still unfolding. With you and the slave singers, "I want to be in that number."

Your friend as ever

NOTES

Preface

1. Paulo Freire, *Pedagogy of the Oppressed* (Continuum ed., 1989), 31.
2. Albert Camus, *Resistance, Rebellion, and Death* (1960), 26.
3. Franz Fanon, *Black Skins, White Masks* (1967), 228–29.
4. Ibid., 187.
5. Ibid., 229 (first emphasis added).
6. *A Testament of Hope: The Essential Writings of Martin Luther King Jr.,* (James Washington, ed. 1986), 313, 314.
7. Robert L. Carter, book review of Mark Tushnet, *The NAACP's Legal Strategy against Segregated Education, Michigan Law Review* 86 (1988): 1083.

Introduction: Divining Our Racial Themes

The epigraph is from Maya Angelou, "I Dare to Hope," *New York Times,* 25 August 1991, 15.

1. Alex Haley, *Roots* (1976); see John Hope Franklin and Alfred A. Moss, *From Slavery to Freedom,* 6th ed. (1988), 425 (calling *Roots* "one of the most successful and fascinating works of this period").
2. William Wiecek, *Sources of Antislavery Constitutionalism in America: 1760–1848* (1977), 62–63.
3. David Swinton, "The Economic Status of African Americans: 'Permanent' Poverty and Inequality," in *The State of Black America* (National Urban League, 1991), 25.
4. Ibid. 36–37.

5. Act of 2 July 1964, P.L. 88–352, 42 U.S.C.A. §§2000e-2000e-17.

6. Fair Housing Act of 1968 (1970) (as amended 1988 in §13(a) of Pub. L. 100–430, short title "Fair Housing Amendments Act of 1988).

7. Kimberlè Crenshaw, "Race, Reform, and Retrenchment: Transformation and Legitimation in Antidiscrimination Law," *Harvard Law Review* 101 (1988): 1331, 1380–81.

8. Edmund Morgan, *American Slavery, American Freedom* (1975), 8.

9. Derrick Bell, "The Racial Imperative in American Law," in *The Age of Segregation: Race Relations in the South, 1890–1945* (1978).

10. Herbert Hill, *Black Labor and the American Legal System* (1977); William Gould, *Black Workers in White Unions* (1977).

11. Kevin Phillips, *The Politics of Rich and Poor* (1990).

12. bell hooks, *Feminist Theory from Margin to Center* (1984), 54.

13. Gunnar Myrdal, *An American Dilemma* (1944), xix.

14. Ibid.

15. Jennifer Hochschild, *The New American Dilemma* (1984), 203.

16. Ibid., 5.

17. Ibid.

18. Linda Myers, *Understanding an Afrocentric World View: Introduction to an Optimal Psychology* (1988), 8.

19. Ibid.

20. Ibid.

21. Orlando Patterson, *Slavery and Social Death* (1982), 76.

22. Ernest Becker, *The Denial of Death* (1973), 11–12.

Chapter 1: Racial Symbols: A Limited Legacy

The epigraph is from Langston Hughes, "Puzzled," in *Selected Poems of Langston Hughes* (1990), p. 191.

1. See for example, Langston Hughes, *The Best of Simple* (1961).

2. *Encyclopaedia Britannica* (1977), V, 187.

3. National Urban League, *The State of Black America 1984* (1984), 151.

4. John Hope Franklin and Alfred A. Moss, *From Slavery to Freedom,* (ed. 6th 1988), 444.

5. Langston Hughes, "Mother to Son," in *Don't You Turn Back: Poems by Langston Hughes,* Lee Bennett Hopkins, ed. (1967), 20.

6. Mark Costello and David Foster Wallace, *Signifying Rappers: Rap and Race in the Urban Present* (1990).

7. John Edgar Wideman, preface, *Breaking Ice: An Anthology of Contemporary African-American Fiction* (1990), v-x.

8. *Brown v. Board of Education*, 349 U.S. 294, 301 (1955) (returning the cases to the district courts with the admonition that orders and decrees be entered to admit plaintiffs to public schools on a racially nondiscriminatory basis "with all deliberate speed ...").

9. Patricia Williams, "Alchemical Notes: Reconstructing Ideals from Deconstructed Rights," in *A Less Than Perfect Union: Alternative Perspectives on the United States Constitution*, J. Lobel, ed. (1988), 56.

10. Ibid., 64.

11. Toni Morrison, *Beloved* (1988), 244.

12. "City Called Heaven," *Songs of Zion* (1981), 135.

Chapter 2: The Afrolantica Awakening

The epigraph is from Julius Lester, "The Necessity for Separation," *Ebony*, August 1970, pp. 166–69.

1. Bergen Evans, *Dictionary of Mythology* (1970), 36.

2. *City of Richmond v. J. A. Croson Co.*, 488 U.S. 469 (1989) (ruling that policies intended to remedy past discrimination must be adjudged by the same strict scrutiny standards previously applied only to invidious racial classifications).

3. See Derrick Bell, *Race, Racism, and American Law*, 1st ed. (1973), 114–17.

4. S. Harris, *Paul Cuffe: Black America and the African Return* (1972).

5. W. Foster, *The Negro People in American History* (1954), 173.

6. John Hope Franklin and Alfred Moss, *From Slavery to Freedom*, 6th ed. (1988), pp. 320–22. See also E. Fax, *Garvey* (1972); E. Cronon, *Black Moses: The Story of Marcus Garvey and the Universal Negro Improvement Association* (1969); Marcus Garvey, *Philosophy and Opinions of Marcus Garvey*, A. Garvey, ed., 2d ed. (1968).

7. Franklin and Moss, *From Slavery*, 322.

8. The authorities are collected in E. Osofsky, *Come Out From Among Them: Negro Migration and Settlement, 1890–1914* (1966); see also, Nicholas Lemann, *The Promised Land* (1991).

9. Franklin and Moss, *From Slavery*, 189.

10. Ibid.

11. Vincent Harding, *There Is a River* (1983), 154.

12. See Arna Bontemps and Jack Conroy, *Anyplace But Here* (1945); G. Groh, *The Black Migration* (1972); and Lemann, *The Promised Land* (1991).

13. *Wallace v. Brewer,* 315 F. Supp. 431 (M.D. Ala. 1970).

14. *New York Times,* 17 May 1970, p. 32, col. 2.

15. Edwin Redkey, *Black Exodus* (1969), 32.

16. Leon Litwack, *North of Slavery: The Negro in the Free States, 1790–1860* (1961), 259.

Chapter 3: The Racial Preference Licensing Act

The epigraph is from Matthew S. Goldberg, "Discrimination, Nepotism, and Long-Run Wage Differentials," *Quarterly Journal of Economics* 97 (1982): 307.

1. *Plessy v. Ferguson,* 163 U.S. 537 (1896) (upholding statute requiring segregated railway coaches).

2. *Havens Realty Co. v. Coleman,* 455 U.S. 363 (1982).

3. Civil Rights Act of 1964, 42 U.S.C. Secs. 1971, 1975a-1975d, 2000a-2000h-6 (1988).

4. Civil Rights Act of 1991, Public Law No. 102-166, 105 Stat. 1071 (1991).

5. See, for example, *Heart of Atlanta Motel, Inc. v. United States,* 379 U.S. 241 (1964), and *Katzenbach v. McClung,* 379 U.S. 294 (1964) (both cases upholding the public facilities provisions of Title II).

6. Fair Housing Act of 1968, Pub. L. 90–284, Title VIII, sections 801–19, 42 U.S.C. SS 3601–19 (1970) (as amended 1988, Section 13(a) of Pub. L. 100-430, short title "Fair Housing Amendments Act of 1988").

7. *Brown v. Board of Education,* 347 U.S. 483 (1954).

8. See *City of Richmond v. J. A. Croson Co.,* 488 U.S. 469 (1989).

9. *Brown v. Board of Education II,* 349 U.S. 294 (1955).

10. Alexander Bickel, *The Least Dangerous Branch: The Supreme Court at the Bar of Politics* (1962), 247–54.

11. Derrick Bell, "Serving Two Masters: Integration Ideals and Client Interests in School Desegregation Litigation," *Yale Law Journal* 85 (1976): 470.

12. Comment, "Brown v. Board of Education and the Interest-Convergence Dilemma," *Harvard Law Review* 93 (1980): 518.

13. See Derrick Bell, *Race, Racism, and American Law,* 2nd ed. (1980), 2–44.

14. Ibid., 33.

15. Gary Becker, *The Economics of Discrimination*, 2nd ed. (1971). See, for example, Richard Epstein, *Forbidden Grounds: The Case Against Employment Discrimination Laws* (1992); Richard A. Posner, *Economic Analysis of Law*, 3rd ed. (1986), 621–23; John J. Donohue, "Is Title VII Efficient?" *University of Pennsylvania Law Review* 134 (1986): 1411; Richard A. Posner, "The Efficiency and Efficacy of Title VII," *University of Pennsylvania Law Review* 136 (1987): 513; John J. Donohue, "Further Thoughts on Employment Discrimination Legislation: A Reply to Judge Posner," *University of Pennsylvania Law Review* 136 (1987): 523; and Strauss, "Law and Economics." See also John J. Donohue and Peter Siegelman, "The Changing Nature of Employment Discrimination Litigation," *Stanford Law Review* 43 (1991): 983; John J. Donohue and James J. Heckman, "Re-Evaluating Federal Civil Rights Policy," *Georgetown Law Journal* 79 (1991): 1713.

16. Donohue, "Is Title VII Efficient?" 1411–12.

17. Posner, "Efficiency and Efficacy of Title VII," 513, 521.

18. Ibid., 516.

19. David A. Strauss, "The Law and Economics of Racial Discrimination in Employment: The Case for Numerical Standards" *Georgetown Law Journal* 79 (1991): 1619, 1630.

20. Matthew Goldberg, "Discrimination, Nepotism, and Long-Run Wage Differentials," *Quarterly Journal of Economics* 97 (1982): 307.

21. See *Economic Report of the President*, H.R. Doc. No. 28, 92d Cong., 1st Sess. 119 (1971).

22. See Conn. Gen. Stat. Sec. 22a–6b (West Supp. 1990).

23. Act of 7 August 1977, Pub. L. No. 95–96, 91 Stat. 714, codified as amended at 42 U.S.C. Sec. 7420(2)(A) (1988 & Supp. 1990).

24. Act of 7 August 1977, as amended at 42 U.S.C. Sec. 7503(1)(A) (1988).

25. "There's Another Way to Honor King," *Chicago Tribune*, 18 November 1990, sec. 4, p. 3.

26. George Will, "Bush's Blunder on Racial Scholarships," *Newsday* 27 December 1990, p. 95 (characterizing Fiesta Bowl officials' actions as a "penance for the sin of playing football in Arizona").

27. See Nell Painter, *Standing at Armageddon: The United States, 1877–1919* (1987), 110–40, 163–69.

28. Herbert Wechsler, "Toward Neutral Principles of Constitutional Law," *Harvard Law Review* 73 (1959): 1 (suggesting that the *Brown*

decision may have arbitrarily traded the rights of whites not to associate with blacks in favor of the rights of blacks to associate with whites).

29. For a summary of black reparations efforts in both the nineteenth and the twentieth centuries, see Bell, *Race, Racism,* 44–47.

30. Herbert Wechsler, "Toward Neutral Principles," *Harvard Law Review* 73 (1959): 1, 34.

31. *The Tales of Uncle Remus: The Adventures of Brer Rabbit,* Julius Lester, ed. (1987), 10, 15–16.

Chapter 4: The Last Black Hero

1. "What's Love Got to Do with It," by Terry Britten/Graham Lyle, Myaxe Music, Ltd., 1984. Recorded by Tina Turner on album, "Private Dancer," Capitol-EMI, ST-12330 (1983).

Chapter 5: Divining a Racial Realism Theory

1. James H. Cone, *Martin & Malcolm & America* (1991), 207.

2. See Eric Foner, *Reconstruction: America's Unfinished Revolution 1863–1877* (1988); W. E. B. Du Bois, *Black Reconstuction in America* (1981); and C. Vann Woodward, *Reunion and Reaction* (1981).

3. For a good explication of realism's roots, see Edward A. Purcell, Jr., "American Jurisprudence Between the Wars: Legal Realism and the Crisis of Democratic Theory," in Lawrence M. Friedman and Harry N. Scheiber, eds., *American Law and the Constitutional Order* (1988), 359–63. See also Kermit L. Hall, *The Magic Mirror in American History* (1989), p. 269.

4. See Hall, *Magic Mirror,* 269.

5. *Coppage v. Kansas,* 236 U.S. 1 (1915) (finding the due process clause protected the right of workers to contract with their employees without interference by the state).

6. See Elizabeth Mensch, "The History of Mainstream Legal Thought," in David Kairys, ed., *The Politics of Law,* rev. ed. (1989) 13, 20.

7. G. Edward White, "From Realism to Critical Legal Studies: A Truncated Intellectual History," *Southwestern Law Journal* 40 (1986): 819, 821.

8. Roscoe Pound, "Law in Books and Law in Action," *American Law Review* 44 (1910), 12.

9. Arthur S. Miller, "Pretense and Our Two Constitutions," *George Washington Law Review* 54 (1986): 375. This thesis is developed at length in Arthur S. Miller, *The Secret Constitution and the Need for Constitutional Change* (1987).

10. *Regents of the University of California v. Bakke*, 438 U.S. 265 (1978) (upheld the use of race as a consideration in educational admissions decisions).

11. Elizabeth Mensch, "The History of Mainstream Legal Thought," in David Kairys, ed., *The Politics of Law*, rev. ed. (1989), 13, 21.

12. Ibid., 21.

13. Ibid., 23–24.

14. Ibid., 23.

15. See Anita Allen, "Legal Philosophy," in Stephen Gillers, ed., *Looking at Law School* (1990), 305 (drawing connections between legal realism and critical race theory).

16. Purcell, Jr., "American Jurisprudence," 359, 362.

Chapter 6: The Rules of Racial Standing

1. Langston Hughes, "Note on Commercial Theatre," in *Selected Poems of Langston Hughes* (1990), 190.

2. "Encouragement," in *The Complete Poems of Paul Lawrence Dunbar* (1970), 296.

3. *Valley Forge Christian College v. Americans United*, 454 U.S. 464, 472 (1982) (organization dedicated to separation of church and state failed to identify any personal injury suffered by them as consequence of alleged constitutional error in transfer of federally owned property to religious organization without financial payment therefor).

4. Actually, the standing doctrine has often served as a barrier for blacks seeking relief from undeniable racial abuse: for example, in *Allen v. Wright*, 468 U.S. 737 (1984), the Court denied standing to black parents who contended that the Internal Revenue Service had not carried out its obligation to deny tax-exempt status to private schools practicing discrimination based on race as approved the year before in *Bob Jones University v. United States*, 461 U.S. 574 (1983). The Court in *Allen* cited *O'Shea v. Littleton*, 414 U.S. 488 (1974); *Rizzo v. Goode*, 423 U.S. 362 (1975); and *City of Los Angeles v. Lyons*, 461 U.S. 95 (1983). In these cited cases, plaintiffs sought injunctive relief against systemwide law

enforcement practices, but were denied standing for failing to allege a specific threat of being subjected to the challenged practices.

5. Ralph Ellison, *Invisible Man* (1947).

6. See *Batson* v. *Kentucky*, 476 U.S. 79 (1986) (enabling a criminal defendant to make out a prima-facie case of jury discrimination solely on the evidence concerning the prosecutor's exercise of the peremptory challenges at the defendant's trial).

7. *Commonwealth of Pennsylvania* v. *Local Union 542, International Union of Operating Engineers*, 388 F. Supp. 155 (E. D. Pa. 1974).

8. *Brown* v. *Board of Education*, 347 U.S. 483 (1954) (holding segregated schools unconstitutional).

9. Richard Kluger, *Simple Justice* (1975).

10. David Garrow, *Bearing the Cross: Martin Luther King, Jr., and the Southern Christian Leadership Conference* (1986); David J. Garrow, *The FBI and Martin Luther King, Jr.* (1983).

11. Taylor Branch, *Parting the Waters: America in the King Years, 1954–63* (1988).

12. Philip H. Melanson, *The MURKIN Conspiracy: An Investigation into the Assassination of Dr. Martin Luther King, Jr.* (1989). Other important biographies include James A. Colaiaco, *Martin Luther King, Jr., Apostle of Militant Nonviolence* (1988); and Lionel Lokos, *House Divided: The Life and Legacy of Martin Luther King* (1968).

13. James H. Cone, *Martin & Malcolm & America* (1991); Vincent Harding, *Hope and History* (1990); Bernard C. Watson, *We Shall Overcome: Martin Luther King, Jr., and the Black Freedom Struggle* (1990); C. Eric Lincoln, *Martin Luther King, Jr.: A Profile* (1985); Vincent Harding and Walter E. Fluker, *They Looked for a City* (1989); David L. Lewis, *King: A Biography* (1978); Lerone Bennett, Jr., *What Manner of Man: A Biography of Martin Luther King, Jr.* (1968); Louis E. Lomax, *To Kill a Black Man* (1968); and L. D. Reddick, *Crusader Without Violence: A Biography of Martin Luther King, Jr.* (1959).

14. Gloria Joseph, "The Incompatible Ménage à Trois: Marxism, Feminism, and Racism," cited in bell hooks, *Feminist Theory: From Margin to Center* (1984), 51.

15. bell hooks, *Yearning: Race, Gender, and Cultural Politics* (1990), 11.

16. See Randall Kennedy, "Racial Critiques of Legal Academia," *Harvard Law Review* 102 (1989): 1745.

17. See, for example, Randall Kennedy, "Race Relations Law and the Tradition of Celebration: The Case of Professor Schmidt," *Columbia*

Law Review 86 (1986): 1622; "Commentary: Persuasion and Distrust: A Comment on the Affirmative Action Debate," *Harvard Law Review* 99 (1986): 1327; "Colloquy: A Reply to Philip Elman," *Harvard Law Review* 100 (1987): 1938; "McCleskey v. Kemp: Race, Capital Punishment, and the Supreme Court," *Harvard Law Review* 101 (1988): 1388.

18. Charles Rothfeld, "Minority Critic Stirs Debate on Minority Writing," *New York Times,* 5 January 1990, sec. B, p. 6, col. 3

19. Stephen L. Carter, *Reflections of an Affirmative Action Baby* (1991).

20. Ntozake Shange, *For colored girls who have considered suicide when the rainbow is enuf* (1975).

21. For a discussion of the criticism surrounding Alice Walker's 1982 book, *The Color Purple,* particularly criticism of the Steven Spielberg film based on the book, see bell hooks, *Yearning* (1990), 70–71, 176–79. See also Jack Matthews, "Three Color Purple Actresses Talk About Its Impact," *Los Angeles Times,* 31 January 1986, sec. 6, p. 1; Jack Matthews, "Some Blacks Critical of Spielberg's Purple," *Los Angeles Times,* 20 December 1985, sec. 6, p. 1; Clarence Page, "Toward a New Black Cinema," *Chicago Tribune,* 12 January 1986, sec 5, p. 3.

22. I Samuel 17:46.

23. Sam Roberts, "Blacks and Jews in New York Condemn Farrakhan's Views," *New York Times,* 4 October 1985, p. A1, col. 2.

24. Ibid.

25. Ibid.

26. Lucius J. Barker, *Our Time Has Come: A Delegate's Diary of Jesse Jackson's 1984 Presidential Campaign* (1988), 62–87.

27. Bernard Weinraub, "Reagan Joins Kohl in Brief Memorial at Bitburg Graves," *New York Times,* 6 May 1985, p. A1.

28. hooks, *Yearning,* 11.

29. Nancy Lawson, "Paradise Revised: Development of a Drug-Free Success Story," *Washington Times,* 5 July 1991, sec. B, p. 3.

30. Stephen L. Carter, *Reflections of an Affirmative Action Baby* (1991).

31. Lucius J. Barker, *Our Time Has Come* (1988), 84.

Chapter 7: A Law Professor's Protest

The epigraph is from John Newton's "Amazing Grace," *Songs of Zion* (1981), 211.

1. Harvard's Affirmative Action Plan (Spring 1988).

2. Ibid.

3. Richard Chused, "The Hiring and Retention of Minorities and Women on American Law School Faculties," *University of Pennsylvania Law Review* 137 (1988), 537, 538–39.

4. This data was obtained from the academic deans during the meetings on which the Association's report is based. For a more detailed review of this data and the deans' explanations for the small number of minority faculty, see Derrick Bell, "The Final Report: Harvard's Affirmative Action Allegory," *Michigan Law Review* 87 (1989): 2382.

5. W. E. B. Du Bois, *The Seventh Son: The Thought and Writings of W. E. B. Du Bois* (1971), vol. I (J. Lester, ed.), 385.

6. This 31 December 1988 letter from Professor Robert Paul Wolff to the author was published in Derrick Bell, "The Final Report: Harvard's Affirmative Action Allegory," 87 *Michigan Law Review* (1989), 2382, 2405. Reprinted with permission.

7. Mari Matsuda, "Affirmative Action and Legal Knowledge: Planting Seeds in Plowed-Up Ground," *Harvard Women's Law Journal* 11 (1988): 1, 8.

8. See *Commonwealth of Pennsylvania* v. *Local Union 542, International Union of Operating Engineers,* 388 F., Supp. 155 (E.D. Pa. 1974). Judge Leon Higginbotham denied the defendant union's motion that he recuse himself from hearing a civil rights case. The motion alleged personal bias because of the judge's reputation as a black scholar in race relations and his presentation of a pro–civil rights speech to a mainly black historians' association that did not mention the defendants or the case.

9. Robert Williams, University of Arizona Law School; Angela Harris, University of California at Berkeley Law School, Kimberlè Crenshaw and Mari Matsuda, UCLA Law School; Jerome Culp, Duke Law School; Richard Delgado, University of Colorado Law School; Gerald Torres, Minnesota Law School; Lani Gunier, University of Pennsylvania Law School; Charles Lawrence, Stanford Law School. Other minority teachers whose writings reflect critical race theory influences include Paulette Caldwell and Peggy Davis, NYU Law School; Linda Greene and Patricia Williams, Wisconsin Law School; Harlan Dalton, Yale Law School; Kendall Thomas, Columbia Law School; Dwight Green, Hofstra Law School; Girardeau Spann, Georgetown University Law School.

10. See, for example, Mari J. Matsuda, "When the First Quail Calls: Multiple Consciousness as Jurisprudential Method," *Women's Rights Law Reports* 11 (1989): 7; Jerome Culp, "Toward a Black Legal Scholarship: Race and Original Understandings," *Duke Law Journal* (1991):

39 (legal scholarship remains one of the last vestiges of white supremacy in civilized intellectual circles); Angela Harris, "Race and Essentialism in Feminist Legal Theory," *Stanford Law Review* 42 (1990), 581, 586 ("My suggestion is only that we make our categories explicitly tentative, relational, and unstable, and that to do so is all the more important in a discipline like law, where abstraction and 'frozen' categories are the norm"); Richard Delgado and Jean Stefancic, "Why Do We Tell the Same Stories?: Law Reform, Critical Librarianship, and the Triple Helix Dilemma," *Stanford Law Review* 42 (1989), 207, 219–20 (criticizing the absence of combined references for race *and* gender discrimination in law indices); Deborah King, "Multiple Jeopardy, Multiple Consciousness: The Content of a Black Feminist Ideology," *Signs* 14 (1988), 272, 295, (arguing for a multivalent, interactive pedagogical model of categorization to capture black women's consciousness, instead of the traditional additive analysis where black women's consciousness is shaped by race *plus* sex or vice versa); Kimberlè Crenshaw, "Demarginalizing the Intersection of Race and Sex: A Black Feminist Critique of Antidiscrimination Doctrine, Feminist Theory, and Antiracist Politics," *University of Chicago Law Forum* (1989).

11. "Dissatisfied Women and Minorities: Dire Predictions of a Mass Exodus Prove Unfounded," *National Law Journal* (28 May 1990): S9. (The study showed that more than half [52 percent] of the black lawyers surveyed said they planned to change their legal environment.)

12. James Bennet, "Thieving Lawyers Draining Client Security Funds," *New York Times,* 27 December 1991, B16, col. 3.

13. Psalms 96, 98, and 149.

14. Isaiah 42:10.

Chapter 8: Racism's Secret Bonding

1. Frederick Douglass, speech at Rochester, N.Y., 5 July 1852, in Carter G. Woodson, ed., *Negro Orators and Their Orations* (1925), 197, 209.

2. Kimberlè Crenshaw, "Race, Reform, and Retrenchment: Transformation and Legitimation in Antidiscrimination Law," *Harvard Law Review* 101 (1988): 1331, 1380–81.

3. Toni Morrison, "The Pain of Being Black," *Time,* 22 May 1989, p. 120.

4. Jennifer Hochschild, *The New American Dilemma* (1984), 5.

5. Ursula K. Le Guin, "The Ones Who Walk Away from Omelas," in *The Wind's Twelve Quarters* (1975), 281–82.

6. bell hooks, *Feminist Theory from Margin to Center* (1984), 54.

7. Andrew Hacker, "The World According to Andrew Hacker," *Amherst,* Fall 1991, 8, 12.

8. Ralph Ellison, "What America Would Be Like Without Blacks," in Ralph Ellison, *Going to the Territory* (1986), 104, 111.

9. Ibid., 112.

10. Ibid., 111.

Chapter 9: The Space Traders

1. See John Yewell, Chris Dodge, and Jan Desirey, eds., *Confronting Columbus: An Anthology* (1992).

2. Military Selective Service Act, 50 USCS Appx §451, et seq. See, for example, *Selective Draft Law Cases,* 245 U.S. 366 (1918).

3. L. Levy, K. Karst, and D. Mahoney, eds., *Encyclopedia of the American Constitution,* II (1986), 761.

4. Langston Hughes, "Note on Commercial Theatre," in *Selected Poems of Langston Hughes* (1990), 190.

5. John Newton, "Amazing Grace," in *Songs of Zion* (1981), 211.

6. Lucy S. Dawidowicz, *The Holocaust and the Historians* (1981); Lucy S. Dawidowicz, ed., *A Holocaust Reader* (1976); Asher Cohen, Joav Gelber, and Chad Ward, eds., *Comprehending the Holocaust: Historical and Literary Research* (1988); Judith Miller, *One, By One, By One: Facing the Holocaust* (1988); Yehuda Bauer, *The Holocaust* (1978).

7. David Savage, "1 in 4 Young Blacks in Jail or in Court Control, Study Says," *Los Angeles Times,* 27 February 1990, sec. A, p. 1, col. 1.

8. Jason DeParle, "42% of Young Black Men Are in Capital's Court System," *New York Times,* 18 April 1992, sec. A, p. 1, col. 1.

9. *Luther* v. *Borden,* 48 U.S. (7 How.) 1 (1849) (Court refused to determine which was the legitimate government of Rhode Island).

10. See *Baker* v. *Carr,* 369 U.S. 186 (1962) (exploring the "political question" doctrine in definitive fashion).

11. *Korematsu* v. *United States,* 323 U.S. 214 (1944) (sustaining a military order under which Americans of Japanese origin were removed from designated West Coast areas). See also *Hirabayashi* v. *United States,* 320 U.S. 81 (1943) (upholding a military curfew imposed on persons of Japanese ancestry in the West Coast during the early months of the Second World War).

12. *Giles* v. *Harris,* 189 U.S. 475 (1903).

13. Ibid., 488.

14. See Derrick Bell, "The Referendum: Democracy's Barrier to Racial Equality," *Washington Law Review* 54 (1978):1.

Epilogue: Beyond Despair

1. See Donald L. Robinson, *Slavery in the Structure of American Politics, 1765–1820* (1971), 286 (discussing the Fugitive Slave Act of 1793, which, while including severe penalties for those assisting escaping slaves, "prescribed no penalties for those who sought to kidnap and re-enslave freed Negroes"); Solomon Northrup, *Twelve Years a Slave,* Sue Eakin and Joseph Logsdon, eds. (1968) (real-life autobiography of a free man kidnapped in New York and sold into slavery, where he spent twelve years until his wife successfully petitioned for his release).

2. Nathan Huggins, *Black Odyssey* (1990) 244 (italics added).

3. Ibid., xvi.

4. Ibid., xiii.

5. Ibid., lvi.

6. Ibid., lxxiv.

7. Ibid.

8. Irvin Yalom, *Love's Executioner & Other Tales of Psychotherapy* (1989), 12.

9. Erin Edmonds, "Civil Rights According to Derrick Bell," unpublished manuscript.

Index

Derrick Bell, 1930–2011, was a civil rights attorney, pioneering legal scholar, professor, and political activist. A full-time visiting professor at New York University Law School for over two decades, he was previously the first tenured African American professor on the faculty of Harvard Law School and the first African American dean of the University of Oregon School of Law. He is also the author of *And We Are Not Saved* and several other books.

Michelle Alexander is the acclaimed author of *The New Jim Crow: Mass Incarceration in the Age of Colorblindness* and a visiting professor at Union Theological Seminary.